CW01095708

The S
Of June

A Collection of
Short Stories

 Rainbows Publishing

The rights of Rosemarie Ford, Patricia Golledge, Peter Goodsall, Deborah Grice, Alyson Heap, Martin Mickleburgh, Peter Owen and David Mills to be identified as Authors of the Work has been asserted by them in accordance with the Copyright, Designs and Patents Act 1988.

First published in Great Britain by Rainbows Publishing in 2004

All right reserved. No part of this publication may be reproduced, stored in a retrieval system, or transmitted, in any form or by any means without the prior written permission of the copyright owners.

A catalogue record is available
For this title from the British Library
ISBN 0 954823 51 6

Published in Great Britain by
Rainbows Publishing
Weston-Super-Mare
Somerset

www.rainbows-publishing.co.uk

Copyright © 2004

Contents

Acknowledgements

We are deeply indebted to Stephen Troth for the beautiful cover illustration and for the Pier Group logo.

Also, very many thanks to our guiding light, a teacher who has fired within us the joy of writing!

Thanks also go to Clevedon Pier Trust for allowing us to use their photograph and to Hilary Semens for her help in dealing with some of the more esoteric problems of publishing the book.

The Pier Group

Forward

Having *this* collection of students in the same class was the Creative Writing Tutor's equivalent of striking gold. I often forgot to mark: I was too engrossed in the stories. Talent, determination and a professional attitude towards accepting criticism from their peers made this class turn themselves into a serious writing group and now they've produced this anthology, a highly original collection.

Loss, love, madness – and bananas – it's all here. We hope you will read – enjoy – and be moved.

Deborah Grice
On behalf of
"The Pier Group"

The Shrinking Man

He liked June mornings, he liked the smell of them.
May mornings smelled damp, like the smell of wet earth in basements.

July mornings were too confident, too sure of their place in the hierarchy of summer.

Even worse were August mornings with their oppressive, stagnant heat, smelling of lethargy and languid inevitability.

A June morning smelled as fresh as the corsage on the gown of a young girl at her first grown-up ball.

Only in the early mornings did he experience these odours, as he sat waiting for the high street to wake, shutters springing open like a hundred metal eyelids. Then came the sounds, gentle at first, rising from a dull drone to a symphony of urban percussion.

John Wilde lived in a doorway sandwiched between an off-license and a Laundromat. His space was lined with cardboard, his worldly goods contained in a knapsack and a battered leather hold-all, stacked neatly in a corner. This bijou residence had been his home for five years. His clothes, their once respectable labels unreadable, seemed to be growing bigger as the man inside them was becoming smaller. He used to think that he would die of shame, now he believed that he would simply shrink away and all that would be left of the man he once was would be a pile of clothes with blank labels.

Some passers-by saw through the façade, glimpsed the elegant hands beneath the grime, hands that had once held china tea cups filled with pale tea, hands that had shaken the limp hand of academia in oak panelled vestibules. They noted the neatness of his doorway, echoes of a past life lived with order and purpose. Some quickened their pace, unwilling to dawdle near the man that they might become. Some dropped coins, gestures of kindness amongst the acts of betrayal.

At 8:35 a.m. each weekday morning, people spilled out from the railway station at the end of the High Street like pips bursting from a ripe pomegranate. The black specks made their way to their final destinations, discarding the detritus of their journeys into the open mouths of rubbish bins, greedy for sustenance. From these bins, John Wilde had his pick of daily newspapers. He hoarded them, the tabloids for warmth and insulation, the broadsheets for information and affirmation that the shrinking man could still think. He had never slipped into the passive role of vagrant. As he greedily scanned the papers for news and academic articles, he retained the part of him that was Honours Graduate, respected teacher, scholar and family man.

And so this was his life, a gradual progression from member of the human race to onlooker.

His nightmare had begun on a June day, much like the one he was now celebrating, with its fresh promising smell of summer.

On Monday the sixth of June he began his day, as usual, with the short walk to school. It was a pleasant walk along a tree-lined avenue, the early morning sun glinting through the leaves dappling the pavement in front of him like a carpet of stepping-stones. The imposing wrought iron gates were open and his feet made a satisfying crunch as he made his way along the gravel driveway to the school that had been his place of work for thirty years.

As he entered the hallway he saw the Headmaster, a grim expression on his normally jovial face.

"Ah, John, come to my office please", his tone formal and cold.

John had no inkling of what was to come, indeed he even smiled to himself, thinking there was probably a simple explanation for the Head's gloom, news of an Ofsted inspection perhaps, always guaranteed to strike fear into the heart of a school. He gestured for John to sit in the brown leather armchair opposite his own seat at the desk. The Headmaster was uncomfortable: John saw beads of sweat on his upper lip and he seemed loath to look up as he spoke.

"John, we have had a serious allegation made against you by a pupil in the sixth form…" He paused, unsure how to continue.

John was fascinated by the beads of sweat which continued to form on the Headmaster's upper lip. He could remember thinking that if all of the tiny beads of sweat merged there would be a steady trickle down his chin and it would drip onto the polished wood of the desk, and the rivulet would creep along to the edge where it would quiver before falling to the floor. Meanwhile, his heart was pounding in his ears and nausea was rising from his stomach up into his throat. He could taste it.

"Who?" was all he could say, his mind racing to remember an incident, any incident that could have been misconstrued.

The Headmaster looked at the papers in front of him and taking out a handkerchief from his trouser pocket, he wiped the offending lip.

"Pippa Marshall, I have her statement here…"

Pippa Marshall, Pippa Marshall with her shiny satin ball gown and shiny satin skin, her rose corsage the colour of the bloom on her cheek. Run along Pippa, don't be foolish…

"Her statement?"

"Yes John." He looked up, his eyes weary, a hopelessness in his voice.

"Her parents are insisting that I give this to the police. I persuaded them to wait until I could see you and give you the chance to go voluntarily to the station. John, you will need a lawyer."

As John looked across at his friend of many years, he could see his future. They both knew that his career was at an end. Even if he was exonerated, his teaching life was over.

But neither of them could have foreseen the train of events that was to follow. Like a game of dominoes his life fell in neat lines.

The girl was believed, others told tales. An inappropriate remark, a hand on a thigh, his head too close to the scent of youth. He was imprisoned.

He lost his wife, his family, his home, his career, and so the dominoes fell, one after the other.

He came out of prison and sought anonymity miles from his old life, miles from the man he was.

9

Every year as the sixth of June approached he would steel himself for visitors. They would stand at his shoulder, accuser, doubters, punishers, and he would endure again the shame, pain and humiliation.

And so today is the anniversary, a day to be endured. He is sitting in his usual spot, on the step of his doorway, a little smaller than he was yesterday, but bigger than he will be tomorrow.

At 8:35 a.m. as usual, commuters spill out of the station and rush past him. A girl is hurrying along, her mind on a job interview that she is already late for.

She steps awkwardly and her heel snaps. He hears the sound like a bone breaking and he stands, fearful that she may have broken her ankle. He reaches out a hand to steady her and as she turns to look at him, she cries out and backs away. She falls down heavily on the heel-less shoe and loses her balance on the kerb. The motorcyclist sees her too late and his spinning front wheel hits her. She flies in slow motion through the air, past John Wilde who looks on in horror as he sees Pippa Marshall fall to her death beneath the wheels of a lorry.

He is reminded of a saying by the Chinese philosopher Sun Tzu:

"If you sit by the river for long enough, you will see the bodies of your enemies float by."

He sits down on his doorstep, oblivious to the noise around him, and hopes that the prophecy will be fulfilled before he shrinks away into nothingness.

11th January 1950 - 6th June 2004

It's not at all what I expected. To be frank, I thought it would be better organised than this. No one seems to know what's going on. There ought to be someone in charge. In fact, it's incredible that there isn't, given the situation.

When we arrived, there was a ridiculous scene at the gate, with everyone saying, "After you", "No, after you." In the end I took the initiative and went ahead: after all, someone had to go in first.

I wasn't prepared for such crowds when I got inside. To be honest, I thought the numbers would be fairly limited. But the place was thronging with people, it looked like Wembley, or a scene from one of those ghastly rock festivals you see on the television. Lots more space, of course, massive amounts of space, but so many people, more people than I've ever seen before in my whole life, and I've travelled a fair bit. It was horribly clogged up near the entrance, with people looking confused and not knowing where to head for. I was the same myself, of course, because there were no instructions, no signs or anything to tell you what to do.

Being a logical sort of a chap, I decided to look for whoever was in charge, or at least someone with a bit of authority, so I began to walk round the edge of the crowd, looking out for anyone who might be wearing a badge, or some kind of uniform, however unusual. Not that I expected to see police or anyone like that of course, but I thought there would be some kind of 'official' presence, shall we say, given the circumstances. But there was no one. No one official that is: there was no shortage of ordinary people, of all types too, some most surprising, given where we where. I even saw several old men who my children would have referred to as 'wino's' and a great gaggle of young people in the weirdest clothes – hippies I suppose you would call them. People of all nations, as you would expect, of course, but the *types* were astonishing. A huge gang of coloured youths were sitting down just

11

inside the entrance (yes, just sitting down, would you believe!) and they all had those bizarre hairstyles that look like wigs – dreadlocks I think they call them. I would have thought they would have subscribed to something entirely different.

No one seemed to have any clear purpose about them. Some people were just chatting, standing around laughing as if they were at a party, or stretching out on the grass as if they hadn't a care in the world. Others sauntered about looking around curiously, or just wandered about in a confused and gormless way.

I suppose I ought to describe what the place looks like – it's the sort of thing people always want to know. The trouble is, there's very little to say. It's all just the same. Again, I was surprised. I'd expected something special. But it was just the usual grass, trees and sky. Nothing out of the ordinary. A fairly substantial river ran down the middle, getting a bit narrower and faster as it dropped out of sight. It was flanked by heather and gorse; reminded me of Exmoor, as a matter of fact, though not an ice-cream van in sight, of course. In the distance I could make out a purple haze that looked like mountains. I'm not a mountain man, myself. I like a nice, gentle rural landscape; Constable, that sort of thing. Mountains always seem to attract cloud, as far as I can see. Talking of which, there's a surprising amount about – but not the white fluffy kind you would expect. In fact, it actually looks as though it's going to rain. I didn't bring an umbrella, either.

This is ridiculous. It's raining! Everyone's running to stand under the trees. I must say I expected something a bit more sophisticated than this. Surely there must be some indoor accommodation. I shall ask someone.

I attracted the attention of an older chap – about the same age as myself.

"I say, do you know what the arrangements are?"

"Arrangements?"

I don't think he's as intelligent as I thought.

"I mean, do we have places to stay? Houses, or something similar? What are the sleeping arrangements?"

He stared at me, rather rudely I thought, then a grin grew slowly on his face.

"Don't ask me, mate, I've only just arrived meself. There's some gorgeous looking birds here though – I 'ope it's goin' to be free love and that sort of thing."

I couldn't believe my ears. The fellow was quite crude and vulgar. Why had they let in types like that?

He added an afterthought. "Oh, some bloke said there was like tree-houses over there."

Tree houses! What on earth...I didn't expect a mansion, though, actually, one had been led...But tree houses! How primitive could you get? Were we all to live like savages in the jungle, hunting round for roots to eat?

As if he'd read my mind, the uncouth fellow said, "If you're hungry mate, there's all sorts of fruit trees over there." He pointed across the river. "Never tasted apples like it since I were a lad. Plums so juicy it runs down your chin. Goosegogs, raspberries, strawberries – the lot – it's like the bloody Garden of Eden." He smacked his lips appreciatively.

Wincing at his profanity I set off in the direction he had indicated. It was tough-going, zig-zagging through the bracken, and not even a bridge over the river. I had to take my shoes off and *paddle* across. Through the trees on the other side I saw what he'd been referring to – wooden houses built on platforms, right in amongst the leaves. Living in the tree canopy like apes! Surely this was regression. The soul of Man, gradually refining through generations and generations to ever higher levels, to be rewarded with fruit, like a monkey. My indignation boiled over. Was this the reward for all my endeavours, for such a long pilgrimage? Surely I had earned more than this...this glorified outing to the country!

I picked up a branch and began to whack the nearest tree angrily.
"Owww!"

My jaw dropped. It was the tree. The tree had spoken. It was a dream. It had to be. The whole thing was a dream, from beginning to end. Or had I gone mad?

"What's wrong?" It *was* the tree speaking.

"I...I..."my voice faltered (it doesn't come naturally, to speak to a tree). Then I remembered my outrage.

13

"Well, I'm a bit put out, if you'd like to know. This is not what I'd been led to expect."

"Oh, indeed." The tree spoke gravely. "And what did you expect?"

"Oh, I don't know exactly, but something a little more comfortable, if you know what I mean. Even a little…well, luxury, if you must know."

"Streets paved with gold? Palaces made of diamonds?"

"Well, not necessarily that luxurious. But not tree-houses!"

"They are well-appointed: soft beds, warm linings, waterproof."

"What about 'my father's house has many mansions?'"

"Do you know what a metaphor is?"

I frowned. "Something to do with poetry, I think."

"Ah, not a scholar, then."

"I've got five GCE's and two perfectly good A-levels."

The tree smiled. Yes, you heard me: the tree smiled.

"You will find here the most comfortable life you have ever known. It is not what is here, but what is not here that matters. All evil has been removed."

"I heard a man swear! And lust after women!"

The tree laughed so hard that all his leaves shook.

"You have a lot to learn, my son. But don't worry, you have a long time to learn it." He laughed again, his bark wrinkling into a thousand smiling lines. "All eternity." He nudged the next tree with the end of a bough and suddenly the whole wood was shaking with laughter, all the leaves rustling as if a great wind was stirring in it. Chestnuts, beech nuts, dates, coconuts and other missiles dropped all round me, and from a great height, a deep voice boomed out, "Have a banana, son, have a banana."

God guffawed with laughter, and his jovial tears fell like plump drops of monsoon rain onto the bright, leafy canopy of heaven.

Breakfast

I made us your favourite breakfast: soft boiled egg; Marmite soldiers and orange juice. The top of your egg was sliced off to reveal that molten pool of bright liquid that engulfed the slivers of toast that were thrust into it. Yours remained untouched.

I brushed your hair. You always liked having your hair brushed, except when it got caught in the tangles and I pulled too hard, then your yelps and complaints of "you're being too rough" would end in playful squabbling. It looked particularly dark this morning, framing the paleness of your face. You looked no less beautiful.

We had stayed up all night talking, playing your favourite pieces of music and some of mine. We had widely different tastes, only to be expected with the difference in years between us. You were always willing to listen to my 'old fogey music' as you called it, whereas I was always telling you to turn yours down. Tonight though that didn't matter, all that mattered was that we were together.

I held your hand, so delicate within my shovel fingered mitts. You've finally managed to grow your nails; I'll help you paint them. You always liked to wear them black but that doesn't seem appropriate today somehow. I found this bottle in your things, an iridescent purple, you must like it and I think it'll suit today much better.

It was difficult to keep your hand steady, but I don't think I made too much of a hash of it, nail varnish never was my speciality. Remember when I fell asleep one Christmas after lunch? You painted my toenails, each one a different colour. You thought it was hilarious when I woke up and I didn't half take some ribbing down at the gym. But I do enjoy seeing and hearing you laugh: your nose wrinkles and your eyes light up and then you begin to shake and that giggle escapes. Somehow it manages to infect everyone around. You have that ability, spoiling everyone around with love and your

15

non-stop chattering; we always joked that you were born talking. Tonight though I've been doing the talking.

I read to you some of the poems that I've written for you. We can decide which one to read tomorrow. I read to you from the book you're reading, it's called 'Lola Rose' by Jacqueline Wilson. I can't pretend that it makes much sense to me, but then, so long as you enjoy it.

I left the room for a few minutes, I did not want to go, I was afraid that you would leave before I came back. You hadn't.

I spoke of the future, of what you had planned, the places you wanted to visit, the things you wanted to see: turtles laying eggs; giant pandas in bamboo groves; racing kangaroos in the bush; trying to catch an ostrich. And that reminds me of watching you trying to catch snowflakes on your tongue, they never tasted of anything. The look on your face as they instantly disappeared makes me smile even now.

The cold fingers of dawn start to take hold of the sky as I look through the window. There's dew on the grass. It sparkles like jewels as the light strikes it. A fox pauses and looks at me, one paw raised, then continues on his way, soft depressions marking his passing. I go and make our breakfast. The yolk runs down my chin, but this time you don't tut, shake your head or reach forward to wipe it off. I clear away our things and return with a flannel to wipe your face, skin so smooth, unmarked by the stresses of life, eyes once so clear that now stay closed. I pat you dry and I go to shower, shave and dress.

I look at my suit hanging there on the wardrobe door. That isn't right, too sober, too formal, too final. I want to take it down and rip it to pieces, it isn't me and it definitely isn't you, but I don't. I take it down, lay it on the bed and sit next to it, not feeling the energy to move, or the desire to dress.

Slowly and deliberately I pull on the clothes that are a testament to the occasion rather than the person. White shirt, cuffs and collar buttoned; black trousers, crease sharp; shirt tucked in; black socks; black shoes brightly polished; reaching for the black tie my hand pauses and in its stead plucks one with the 'Simpsons' on it. We did after all spend many a meal with trays on our laps giggling at the antics of Springfield's first family.

Then I hear a vehicle pull up outside. I force a gap between the curtains and there it is in all it's black shining splendour. I'd dreamt that when we'd be travelling in a car like this you'd be wearing a dress of white silk and lace, pulling a demure veil across your face and fighting nerves as you prepared to make your life vows; instead it's like this.

Answering the door to the tentative knock I gesture for the men to enter. "Are you ready Mr. Andrews?"

I nod my head and lead them into the front room. Leaning in, I kiss you, my darling daughter, goodbye for the last time and then, as the lid is fastened and that white box is lifted out to the waiting car, the dam breaks. Tears fall soaking my shirt front: I am a man no longer. My reason for living has been taken to rest beside the mother who only knew her for that short week.

Your bravery in your illness made me strong, we supported each other, whose support have I now? Goodbye my rock, only the good die young.

Victoria May Andrews

10th April 1992

6th June 2004

A flame snuffed too soon.

Colin Plank

Colin Plank was born: no doubt about it, the records of Much Grinding-on-the-Moor parish church confirm that to be so. His squat body bore an unusually large head and a pair of shovel-like hands hung limply from the ends of long arms, flicking the ground as his short legs propelled him along with ungainly deportment.

The unfortunate Colin was destined to be ridiculed from an early age. Educated by parents Ruby and Seth at their remote farm high on Exmoor, his early learning had been a painfully slow affair. He was a shy boy able only to conjure up a sheepish grin and a loud snort when approached. The odds seemed stacked against him.

At the age of forty, in spite of everything life had already thrown at him, he started and completed his first novel: 'My Baby She Dun Dun Me No Wrong', in a little under five hours. Since its publication on June 6th 2001, three copies have been snapped up.

In an interview on independent television's 'Legends of Exmoor' programme, Colin stated that the revenue generated from the sales so far would go some way towards the purchase of a second pedal for his bicycle, enthusing that he could soon easily have enough to buy a saddle as well, which he hoped would minimise the distressing effects on his haemorrhoids during the weekly cycle into the village, his backside perched precariously on the stem where a saddle once sat.

During the course of the interview, when asked to describe some of the more memorable moments in his life, Colin looked momentarily perplexed, mouth agape, brow furrowed, before replying sombrely, that once when cycling back from the shops, his baguette got caught up in the front spokes, catapulting him over the handlebars, spread-eagling his mint imperials and crushing his curly-wurly.

"Even better than that," he chuckled, he could also remember the occasion he'd "caught the wrong bus – and had to get off again."

Buoyed by the initial success of his book, he has begun work on a sequel, 'My Baby Up and Left Me'. Now a youthful forty-three, Colin lives happily in a small caravan on the edge of Exmoor, where he is in great demand as an after dinner speaker and singer of folk songs, his gravel-like voice well suited to depicting the harshness of moor-land life. In these often humorous, yet poignant, self penned ditties, he accompanies himself on an old cement mixer, his arm whirling antics invariably bringing the house down.

Colin Plank is a simple soul who spends a great deal of time realigning his National Health toupee, flossing his dentures and practising forward rolls and backward flips. He likes nothing better than to sit on the steps of the caravan playing with pet rabbit Flopsy and thinking about things. With this in mind he is contemplating writing a non-fiction piece under the heading, 'Things I Think About When I'm Playing Around With My Flopsy'.

Colin has also written a small book of poems collectively entitled 'Who Turned The Bloody Lights Out'. This stunningly unusual collection includes the haunting 'Dad's Been Acting Queer', and the beautifully wistful, 'Can y' See Yer Way to Lending Us a Couple of Quid – Just 'Til the Weekend'.

At the age of twenty-one Colin fell in love, from a distance, with slaughter-man's daughter Honoria Shakes. His first sighting of the voluptuous Honoria was at the Bampton summer fete. Colin and his parents had set up a stall in the hope of selling the many strange artefacts he had collected from the moors during his daily meanderings. Several cups of tea into the morning and Colin felt the necessity to visit the comfort cubicle. Making the relevant excuses, he left the stall and set off in search of the Porta-Loo. Following his nose he headed through the crowds, only to discover, much to his dismay, a long, agitated, queue stretching some way ahead of him. Unsure if he could maintain a holding position for too long, he veered off towards a copse of trees well clear of the main arena. It was there his gaze picked out the rotund figure of Honoria. Hidden from sight of the crowds, behind an elderberry bush, the ample Honoria was rising slowly from the crouch position. Colin slipped in behind a tree and watched in awe

20

as she stooped to pull up a pair of khaki shorts. He clearly detected the
reverberations as she forcefully ejected a substantial volume of trapped wind
before waddling off towards the area designated for the 'welly throwing'
contest. Using the same elderberry bush as cover, Colin excitedly relieved
himself, vowing that one day the delightful Honoria would be his and his
alone. He wanted to hold her, cherish her: she could even share his nasal hair
trimmer. He knew, he just knew, that together they would overcome their
shared predicament of loose wind and, even if they didn't, at least they could
enjoy it together – no one need ever know, provided they kept it quiet.

And so it came to pass that on the occasion of the village harvest supper,
Colin made his play for the plumptious Honoria. Fate had placed them on
opposite sides of the well-laden table. Colin fidgeted and fiddled his way
through the meal, constantly glancing across to Honoria in the hope of
catching her eye. His hair-piece, well brushed and sitting squarely on his huge
head; a new set of dentures, a touch on the large side, blessing him with an
almost permanent grin and a pink shirt that retained most of its buttons,
gave Colin an unusual air of confidence. Honoria however, appeared
oblivious to his amorous glances as she munched through the food stacked
high on her plate. It was time for Colin to make a bold decision. Due to
perform a selection of folk songs later in the evening, he knew he must break
free of the shackles that had been holding him back and dedicate a song to
his secret love – surely that would win her heart. Colin's own heart pounded
as he worked through his set, until eventually his big moment arrived.

"My last song is for a maiden…" Colin faltered a little, but recovered
sufficiently to blurt out plaintively, "…for a maiden who is here tonight but
doesn't know it!"

Not quite how Colin had intended the intro to be, but he was on fire
now; there could be no going back. To a tune not dissimilar to Greensleeves,
he began.

"This day for you my yon fair maiden, I've wormed the dog and cleaned
the seat in the outside privvy 'O.'"

Sadly for Colin, this particular lover's lament wasn't moving Honoria as
hoped, his plight deepening during the rousing, high tempo sing-a-long
section.

"He's cleaned the seat, he's wormed the dog, lets gather in the paper for the privvy 'O."

Colin's new dentures, unable to cope with his extreme facial contortions, finally called it a day, clamping firmly together and refusing to continue, portraying him with a fixed Cheshire Cat like grin, bringing an early and unexpected end to his efforts.

Colin's misery was complete on overhearing Honoria exclaiming loudly as the curtain fell, "ole wiggy with the teeth wants shootin'!"

And that, unfortunately, was the beginning and end of Colin's flirtation with the opposite sex. So, if it's a good holiday read that you are looking for, you could do far worse than search out Colin Plank's ground breaking first novel, with the added satisfaction of knowing that, perhaps, your purchase will be the one to produce that second pedal for his bicycle. Priced at £1.75, its seven pages are packed with some words, and is available in most good butchers and haberdashers shops.

The Breakdown

Shelly tilted her face briefly to the ferocious rain, the stinging so fierce on her pale cheeks that for a moment she almost forgot the pain in her arm as he forced it further up her back.

"You're only the bloody cleaner. Who's gonnae gie you the key tae the Giro cupboard." Shane sneered, his fist wrapped now in her hair.

"Naebody. That's the whole point."

He stared at her, his dark eyes dangerous. She knew she was treading a fine line. Shelly had to convince Shane her plan would work, while at the same time making sure he understood it without appearing to mock his lack of intelligence.

"How dae ye ken its no a set up?"

She took the hand that seconds earlier had taken pleasure in her pain. Holding it in both of hers she smiled, she hoped a loving smile, into the gaunt, unshaven face of an addict

"It's simple, now I've been working there a few weeks naebody even looks at me. They'll make mistakes. It's that easy."

He grunted, swung away from her and marched out of the flat. Shelly could see him approach his 'mate' on the corner of the estate. If you didn't know what you were looking for you could have missed the quick exchange of a grubby pink twenty-pound note for a small pristine white package. Shelly sighed. Where had he got the money for that? As she turned away from the window the open kitchen cupboard caught her eye. One box of porridge oats and a packet of prawn crackers sat alone on the shelf. She leant her head against the cupboard door and thanked God, any God that her Auntie was looking after, and feeding, Melanie tonight.

In the dull light of another dreary day, Shelly donned the magician's invisible cloak of nylon apron and yellow duster. They sat at their desks every morning and never saw her as she dusted, tidied and even crawled under their desks removing the rubbish accumulating at their feet. Shelly knew their names only by overhearing their conversations as she swilled their teacups in the tea-room or scrubbed the next cubicle to them in the toilet.

Shelly's job was manual, but not taxing and she had plenty of time to work out her plan. She rinsed off the cloths in the cleaners' cupboard, the bleach stinging her fingers. The main problem would be patience and, of course, Shane. The plan had to be able to go immediately. She would not be able to pick her moment.

As she walked home, the cold rain soaking through her cheap shoes, the old familiar fear rose again in her gut, the heavy, dank fear. Fear of what she would find back at the flat. Tonight there was only peace. Shane had not returned and Melanie was sleeping the sleep of the innocent, tucked in by a loving Aunt. Shelly sat for a long time by Melanie's bed. She wanted so to stroke the small peachy cheek but worried that the calluses on her hands would wake the child.

In a moment Shelly's resolve crystallised into a tangible, tactile thing. She would succeed and Shane would no longer be the chain dragging her further and further into the depths of the maelstrom. She bit her lip till it bled. She would kick free and her lungs would again be full of air free of the taint of corruption.

Fate is a strange, fickle thing and when you are devoid of all hope and your world is a dark place surrounded by demons, where every step takes you further into the darkness, fate will jump out from around the corner as bright and irreverent as a carnival clown and scream.

"Nah-nah, nah-nah, nah."

Fate did just that the next morning. Shelly wheeled her cleaning trolley through the double doors into the main office. She stepped back slightly at the cacophony that greeted her. The whole place was in uproar. Everyone was running around, reaching across desks, and each other, to answer screaming phones.

"What a bloody day for the Central Computer to break down! It would be the Friday after the Bank Holiday when it's the bloody party tonight, too."

The Breakdown

Shelly's heart stopped for a fraction, only to quicken when the enormity of the situation hit. This was it. Now she could put her plan into action. Today, 6 June, would be the day she changed her life.

All day she carried on as normal. Painstakingly, she did not change either her routine or the speed of each task. The plan relied on her still having work to do at five o'clock.

Like a wisp of smoke from a pipe held clasped between leathery lips, she floated unobtrusively round the desks. A benign spirit, swirling the yellow cloth round the piles of paper and the computer screens, picking up dirty teacups with an obsequious nod and a half smile.

The first batch of giro cheques were brought out of the cash office and placed in the middle of a table hastily erected for the purpose. The four juniors then set to work scribbling frantically. Two hundred had to be hand written by four forty-five.

Shelly's plan had needed the element of panic, but the added lure of a party was just icing on the cake. As the clock ticked its slow minutes round and the noise of phones and cheap biros scratching on watermarked paper started to abate, Shelly made another sweep with her cleaning trolley. A quick flick here and a little rub there, a shy "have you dropped this?" Glad they were for her help, yet when questioned later, no one can remember the cleaner being there; or what she had looked like.

The supervisor stood at the door casting a quick eye round the office mentally ticking her list. Heating off – tick, window shut- tick, all cheques, files and trays locked away - tick. Shelly hovered, and like a juvenile gorilla approaching a silverback she lowered her eyes.

"Shall I give it a wee skite round with the Hoover before I finish. It's a bit of a mess."

The supervisor smiled and almost ran to the front door shouting over her shoulder to security that Shelly was just finishing. She at last stood in the cleaners' cupboard, with the fumes from the different half empty bottles combining to create a potent stench.

She changed out of her overalls and emptied the bag on the trolley, throwing the rubbish into the bin and carefully removing the blank giro cheques she had picked up over the course of her day.

Only later when she could see the flat did she allow herself a shiver of delight. She had done it! With her thoughts of a green Utopia free of Shane, Shelly did not see the unmarked police car follow her along the road to the estate.

She sprinted up the stairwell, desperate to see Melanie and smack! collided with Shane. With a shove he propelled her back down the stairs and pinned her by the neck. The graffiti coated brickwork stuck into her shoulder blades.

"Where the bloody hell have you been. There's pigs everywhere." He tried a more conciliatory approach. "Look, doll, am gonnae really need some gear. Got any money?"

For a fleeting moment she just could not get the lie out.

"Gie us some cash", he roared. His fist tightened on her neck almost lifting her off her feet.

"I've done it, I've got them. Shane, Shane?"

He wrenched her bag from her and ripped its insides out. The three carefully rolled up cheques scattered on the, luckily dry, steps. He made a slightly pathetic picture, crawling around on his hands and knees on the stair of a run down housing estate.

Shelly did not move, more terrified than ever of him, now he had what he wanted. He sauntered over to her, smiling.

"Noo, whit is a dapper, well off chap – like me say, doing with a clapped out auld slapper like you, eh? Yer dumped!"

He bounced her head twice off the wall before marching off to try and cash the cheques. It must have been almost thirty minutes before she came to. She fingered the bruises. Back in the flat there was a note from her upstairs neighbour, Linney, saying Melanie was with her and would probably stay to tea and sleep over. Shelly was glad, too often lately Melanie had seen her in this shameful state. Shame was the bitter taste that filled her mouth, along with the blood from the wound where the teeth had split the skin. Standing by the sink she rinsed her mouth with some very fine Russian vodka. She had hidden it in the washing powder so Shane wouldn't find it. The spirit stung the cuts in her mouth, making her eyes water. She giggled, the sound bursting out into a full guffaw. Here she was on a Friday night with a face swollen and bruised, swigging vodka while her drug addict partner had done a runner with their only chance of getting their hands on some real money. Was she mad? Was it shock or hysteria even? No. As if on cue the doorbell rang.

Shelly called as she walked into the hall, "Chief Inspector Brown, how the devil are you?" She almost managed a smile through her cracked lips. "Tell me you got him."

She opened the door and let in a large bald man in a very fine suit.

"Of course we did," he explained as they returned to the kitchen. "The eejit only cashed the first one for three hundred. Didn't you tell him he could only cash them up to a hundred and fifty quid and without the authentication stamp they were worthless?"

His smile was warm as he leant one large muscular thigh on her kitchen table. She reached for the bottle and poured a glass, which he downed in one gulp. Their tumblers clinked together as they both had another vodka. Shelly was suddenly aware that Inspector Brown's eyes were brown as well. They both smiled.

"Timing was spot on though, he even got to the Post Office just before they shut. We'd spoken to the Post Master. He took it like nothing was suspicious. Went straight to his dealer. Him, dealer and supplier in one go. Well done. You did a good job; look like shit now."

The fingers that tipped back her chin were strong, firm and warm on her cheek. He gently wiped off some dried blood.

"Will you be alright?"

Shelly nodded. She watched the detective as he walked through the estate. Just before he got into his car he turned and waved. The sun was setting over the tower blocks opposite. The thick manila envelope held her new life. Money, new house with a housing authority in a more rural setting. Her fingers traced the phone number scribbled on the back of the envelope, a flush stealing up her cheeks.

She turned her head to the reddening sun and took in a huge breath of air – free air.

Is The Battle O'er?

Nancy was exhausted. It was a beautiful day: hot and sunny - really a day for lying on a sun lounger with a good book rather than exploring a castle. However, she had a job to do and she must get on with it. She walked through the huge archway that once housed a drawbridge to keep out marauding armies, touching the ancient stonework of the archway as she passed through.

"How many more thousands of visitors had done the same thing?" she mused, as she walked to the Bear and Clarence Towers to begin her research. Touching the vast stones brought goose flesh to her arms; she put this down to the cooler air blowing through the vast entrance — but was it? She refused a guided tour; she wanted to explore alone. The guide gave her an old fashioned look and obviously was not happy with this young woman wandering round *his* building without him but he reluctantly conceded when she told him she was a student. Nancy felt quite anti-social wanting to be alone but with the best will in the world it was not possible to absorb the atmosphere of ancient buildings when surrounded by tourists from Germany, America and Japan, not to mention the British, who always wanted to chat. It was difficult to contain her admiration for the strength of the building to withstand any outside attack, let alone mutinies from armoured bands within the Castle.

Moving through the ancient corridors in the steps of the original inhabitants, the power of the past coursed through her veins. In the Ghost Tower she was perturbed by the thought of Greville's lonely troubled ghost wandering the building to the end of time. As she emerged into the sunshine from that edifice a chill ran down her spine and she felt the hairs on the back of her neck begin to stand up. Again, she had a peculiar feeling that the past was trying to speak to her.

She moved back into the shade of the huge building and when she started to investigate the living accommodation for the army in Guy's Tower her sense of déjà vu was getting stronger. What was particularly interesting were the small side-rooms from the main chamber. Strangely, she felt she knew the layout of these rooms before entering that area of the building. One was a toilet and the other a bedchamber; she thought she recognised the bed and she could feel her adrenaline level rising as she became more and more excited. "Was this the first 'en suite' ever created?" Nancy wondered and smiled to herself. There seemed to be muttering in the distance. Could she hear the soldiers talking to each other? "Of course not." she thought, "I'm being stupid. It's visitors in the other rooms. My imagination is running away with me again." she reasoned, and tried to put her feet back on the ground. "I'm a logical individual" she told herself; "I don't believe in ghosts and spirits." But she could not rid herself of this feeling that the past was taking over the present.

More mystery came with Caesar's Tower and its dungeon. How many people had been incarcerated and possibly died in the bowels of this building? Voices were calling to her; she could not clear her mind and was beginning to feel quite overcome by this spiritual influence. Yet more accommodation for guards in this huge quatrefoil bastion seemed very familiar to her. She thought she could see a young girl carrying a tray of bread and gruel with a pewter tankard containing strong smelling ale. It occurred to her that, with its prison accommodation, was this Tower built just near the river for defence, a quick escape, or was the reason darker? Was it next to the moat so that unwanted inmates could be disposed of quietly and discreetly in the dark of night? The moat drained to the River Avon and would be fast running most of the time. She shook herself, musing "I'm beginning to think I could write history all over again."

All the Towers and the Castle itself, with its suits of armour, splendid weapons and Tussaud-like displays of life through the ages, kept bringing the past back to Nancy's fertile imagination.

The strength of the buildings and the fine stonework were inspiring. The wonderful construction could only give inspiration to a budding architect, which subject Nancy was studying at Birmingham University. Her degree course was the reason for her visit but she had enjoyed exploring castles and imagining the past since she was a small child; she had preferred this pastime to building sandcastles on a beach in her early years.

As she walked through the Great Hall she saw the huge tables laden with food, the grand clothes and finery of the aristocracy contrasting with the hand to mouth existence of the menials and felt she had been born five hundred years too late.

She had taken many photographs of the buildings for her thesis and now it was time to take a deep breath of fresh air. Her mind was confused. She was having trouble separating the past from the present and she needed a good dose of oxygen to clear her little grey cells. Her wanderings had drawn her back to the Ghost Tower, and as she came out of the main gate she saw a Guide.

"I want to take some photos of the land surrounding the Castle. Can you recommend a good vantage point?" she asked the elderly gentleman.

With a beaming smile he said "If you've a zoom lens I suggest you go up to The Mound over there." His pointing finger indicated what appeared to be a pretty green hillock covered in grass, bushes and the odd tree or two. "It was part of the original Norman castle defences."

Nancy thanked him again and walked to The Mound. Suddenly hunger pangs gripped her. When she looked at her watch it was three o'clock. "Good heavens," she muttered. "No wonder I'm starving".

She must have been talking aloud to herself because a very surprised passer-by smiled and said, "You look hungry!"

Although she laughed, Nancy could feel the colour rising in her cheeks.

The ground was dry because of the hot sunshine and she spread herself out, sorting the camera equipment whilst eating her sandwiches. Time was rolling along and if she wanted a good number of photographs she needed to get on with it. However, she decided to give herself five minutes rest and lay back on the warm ground. Suddenly she heard "Swish, swish, swish" and a great hue and cry. Men were shouting instructions; there was the clatter of metal as soldiers in suits of armour trudged awkwardly over the rough ground, and an arrow whizzed passed her head as she ran for cover. She wanted to rid her head of this cacophony of noise. The bunch of camomile she had been carrying dropped from her fingers in her haste to gain safety: that was the end of the Captain's tea. She'd get a beating for losing the herb but her fear of the battle and being killed made a beating a small price to pay for survival. Men were dropping around her dripping blood from open wounds, and many were dying in front of her screaming in pain. Despite an overwhelming feeling of nausea from fear and the sight of this flowing blood, Nancy thought perhaps she should try to help

31

although she had no idea where to start or what to do. Then she heard a weak voice; "Help, please help me," begged a young man who was only about sixteen years old, the same age as Nancy. He was bleeding from a deep gash in his leg. His face was ashen and he was shaking with shock and fear. Nancy tore off her petticoat and ripped the rough fabric into a bandage.

"It's not very clean," she said. "I'm not due to wash it until next week." She realised how stupid it was to think of such a mundane thing when she was trying to save a man's life.

"If I bind this, d'you think you c'n get up an' lean on me?" she asked worriedly as she bound the wound with all the speed she could muster. "I'm quite strong. I work in the kitchens an' I'm used t' carryin' 'eavy pots an' pans."

He was much taller than her so she put her arm round the young man's waist and tucked her shoulder under his left arm to try to support his left leg, which by now was dangling numbly. Stumbling and falling occasionally Nancy and the young soldier struggled across the rough open ground and finally gained the shelter of the castle wall. The clamour was dying down and the battle seemed to be abating. It was clear that the marauders had lost their bid to storm the Castle but there had been heavy losses on both sides.

As the girl lowered her young patient to the ground as gently as she could she had an overwhelming urge to care for this boy. She did not wish to see him go: a surge of emotion was swelling her heart and making it beat very fast. She wondered if he could feel it throbbing under the arm that was draped round her neck.

"I'll be a prisoner but thanks for your help. I hope I shan't be treated too badly," her patient said. "My name's John of Leominster."

"I'm Nancy. I work in the kitchen cookin' for the army." She paused, realising that he was of noble blood and she was only a very lowly servant. "I'll leave you now. P'raps you c'd 'ide and gain some strength before tryin' to escape." Then she had a second thought. "If you c'n 'ide under that wall over there, I'll bring you food an' drink at nightfall." She crept away not thinking of the danger in which she was placing herself. She had fallen in love with this man at first sight. The tears were flowing down her cheeks, partly due to relief at escaping the battle, and partly because she knew there could be no romantic future for them because of the difference in their social status. Still, she would do all she could to save his life and try to get him out of the Castle grounds in safety. As she walked back to Guy's Tower she planned an entry to Caesar's Tower. She knew that the night-guard fancied her and would help her for one of her favours. Perhaps they could get the young man away by the moat. She sidled up to the guard fluttering her eyelashes at him.

"Oi've go' a proposition for you," she cajoled.

As she woke up Nancy looked at her watch. What a dream! It was nearly five o'clock and she had lost most of the good light. However, she decided to risk a few long distance shots, packed up her equipment and marvelled that nothing had been stolen. As she sat on the bus for the ride home she was surprised by her own imagination. The dream she had experienced that afternoon had surpassed all previous creations she thought.

She dropped the films in for developing on the way home.

"They'll be ready first thing tomorrow," said the shop assistant.

When she went to collect the prints the girl behind the counter informed her, "There must've been something wrong with your camera because somehow, near the end of the film, a black and white image has covered the coloured print."

"Blast" said Nancy crossly. "This is a new camera. It's the first time I've used it." She paid for the developing and went back to the hall of residence. She felt really disappointed that it was one of the scenic pictures that had been affected.

But when she looked closer at the blurred shot of The Mound through a magnifying glass, Nancy felt that her mind had been blown. In contrast to the grass, it's green highlighted by the brightness of the Sun, she saw an obviously panicking young couple: a boy covered in blood in his tattered jerkin; a girl in a rough sackcloth dress bearing signs of her recent ministrations, clinging together in terror.

The Right Time

It was June the 6ᵗʰ, the third June the 6ᵗʰ that year. It was a bright warm day and the clocks were striking seventeen.

Alice awoke with a start. She was the taller of the two sisters, by a couple of inches, and the younger by a couple of years. At their advanced age two years should have meant nothing, but it was still Marjorie who always took the lead.

"Marjorie, wake up. I think it's time."

Her sister roused herself from the armchair, shuffled over to the mantlepiece, and surveyed the extraordinary clock which dominated it. She traced out the position of the hands with one bony finger then said "I think you're right. But we should check it again, just to be sure."

Alice fetched pencils and paper and, on their knees on the floor, the two old ladies began the calculation once more. Three days. But those were real days and had to be converted into their time, or rather, their brother's time.

Seventeen hours to the day. Fifty-three minutes to the hour. One hundred and three seconds to the minute. And a second is as long as it takes to say "one Mississippi".

Soon the paper was covered with numbers. Several times they lost their place and had to begin again.

Every so often the clocks would ring out, marking their erratic time. No-one could remember when their brother had invented it all. What had been a childhood obsession became a baleful presence in his hundreds of clocks, clocks which refused to simply give up the right time but demanded to be absorbed, divined, demanded a tithe of human reckoning in return for their temporal arabesques. Brother and sisters were engulfed in a cloud of time-gone-mad: midday in the middle of the night and snow in August.

Eventually the calculation was done.

Marjorie said "Yes, that's it, the time has come."

"Should we go and look?" asked Alice, finding herself shuddering. What if he was still alive?

Marjorie was business-like. "Yes, let's see, immediately." But she still picked up the poker as she left the room, just in case.

At the top of the stairs Alice paused.

"Do you think we will be found out, Marjorie?"

"Yes, I think it's inevitable."

"And will they forgive us for what we have done?"

Marjorie straightened her back and tipped her chin up. "After what that monster has done to us, how could they not?"

Half-way down the stairs, Marjorie stopped and turned to her sister. "Do you think we should smash all the clocks and replace them with…" Her voice trailed off at the thought of living with real time. Alice said, gently, "Perhaps we could just do without time entirely."

The cellar was pitch-black and smelt of wet brickwork and coal. Marjorie flipped the light switch. In the far corner, handcuffed to an eyebolt on the wall was their brother. He was lying face-down with his free arm stretched out towards the pitcher of water three feet beyond his finger-tips. He was quite obviously dead.

"You shouldn't have done that Marjorie…he knew it was there even though he couldn't see it." But she smiled as she said it. The sisters faced each other.

"Three minutes without air." said Alice.

"Three weeks without food." said Marjorie.

And then in unison "Three days without water."

Full Circle

She wasn't quite like the others. Yes she was rich, yes she was a widow, but she didn't think that she would ever fall for the smart talk, flattery and charm of someone like Rufus.

June was forty-three, left a widow at forty by one of those motorway pile ups that happen as autumn meanders into winter. Her husband, John, had been wealthy, not filthy rich but comfortable enough to know that if he so wished he need never work again. But that wasn't his style. He had no parents living and no siblings; they had never been blessed with children, so June inherited the lot. After several months recovering from the shock of the loss, she sold the large house, bought something smaller and decided to go out and meet people.

Rufus Sebastopol Hinton was thirty-two: he also had money and he enjoyed the pleasures it had brought him. He had fine clothes, a fast car, a director's box at the local Premiership ground. He ate in expensive restaurants and when he didn't have a girl for his arm he bought one. He hadn't made his money through hard work or shrewd investments. You couldn't really say that he had inherited his money (although this is what he had done): it wasn't family money that he had been left. Rufus had obtained his money from a succession of rich widows, so far five, all of whom had died bequeathing it all to him.

After a visit to his bank he had been told that the pot was shrinking. "Time for number six," he said to himself as he slid into the cool leather of his car. He had found three of his previous spouses on the decks of cruise ships: this, he decided, would be the first port of call.

June had tired of the usual crowd. Bridge was all very well but it hardly gave her the chance to meet younger people; the same could be said of dancing, although she found herself getting quite damp after a session with the Salsa and Tango teacher and it wasn't just sweat. W.I. didn't cut it for her and she found the ramblers a little odd to say the least. She decided to get away from it all, a little cruise to rest and re-evaluate her life. A month cruising the Caribbean, through the Panama Canal and up the West Coast, that should do it, "and you never know," she said to herself, "I might get a chance to try out my dancing skills."

Rufus had joined the ship in Panama. He'd found in the past that it was best for the ship to be part way through the voyage as then the passengers had begun to relax. He hadn't had much luck the first few days: all the women that he had met were either too geriatric (and although their deaths would be less unexpected there was always the danger of suspicious relatives), or they were with partners or in groups, something to do with safety in numbers. It was on the third morning that he spotted her.

She was sitting on one of the deck loungers reading. He took a quick glance at the title, 'The Number One Ladies Detective Agency'. He had to admit it was not a novel he knew. He went to the ship's library, they didn't have a copy, nor did the bookshop, but a quick Internet search brought up the bare bones of the tale. He had to say it didn't sound his cup of tea, but nothing ventured and all that.

Making his way back to the deck he found her still there, eyes closed, book fallen to the deck, pages being riffled by the breeze. The lounger to either side showed no sign of occupation so he sat himself down and waited.

While he waited he studied: fingers for signs of jewellery and evidence of manicures; the hair for evidence of tinting; the face for lines, blemishes and make up; the legs for definition and the body for accommodation. He was not discouraged by his first perusal. The nails were well manicured, not overlong or artificial, and just a hint of gloss applied; there was a wedding band, but he wouldn't let that put him off yet. The hair bore a hint of colour, but that in itself wasn't off-putting, and the bronze was more a colour the wearer chose to please themselves. The face had the early creases that gave evidence of a past but showed much promise for the future. The body and legs, well he wouldn't pay for them but they weren't that bad. He called over loudly to a passing waiter causing her to stir.

"Oh I'm so sorry," he apologised, "I didn't mean to wake you. Can I get you a drink to make up for it? What'll you have?"

June was a little flustered, "just an orange juice please."

"Oh nonsense, come on have something more daring. Two daiquiris please."

"No it's too early, please just an orange juice."

"OK two daiquiris and an orange juice please. Hi, I'm Rufus." He held out his hand, which June grasped tentatively, unsure quite how to react to this stranger. He was polite, spoke gently and was smartly dressed; he appeared to be a few years her junior. She smiled to herself: friends had often told her of the rejuvenating properties of a younger lover. He must be comfortably off to be able to afford this trip.

"I'm June, pleased to meet you." She decided she might as well make the most of this encounter, after all this was the first approach she'd had in two weeks, and after the trip was over she didn't have to see him again. She continued the conversation: it was a boost to have attention and she soon found herself flirting.

Rufus allowed himself a smile; it hadn't taken him long to discover this lady was a wealthy widow, just what he was looking for. His mind was decided.

He didn't have a script, he just let the situation develop. It soon became obvious that he was going to have to tell June as near to the truth as possible, but the whole truth would never do. He told her that he had taken the trip to relax after a hard fought divorce from his second wife that had nearly cost him his business. He had managed to hold on to it, but lost the house and Bentley; the first thing he would have to do when he got back would be to find somewhere to live.

There had been no divorce, Bentley or business. Rufus had been made a widower five times: five times he'd inherited large sums of cash from old ladies who had no one left. They'd all been in their sixties and seventies and he liked to think that he had brought them some comfort during their last weeks, even if he had been the cause of their ultimate demise. He was amazed at how easy it had been to get away with it, but different towns and counties didn't cross check.

Different fates had befallen the ladies: two had died tragically on honeymoon, one 'falling' overboard from the cruise ship they had been on. Another he had persuaded to go skiing at sixty-six years old and a horrible fall had left her with a broken hip from which she had never recovered. Another two he had, over time, altered the dose of their various medications and the fifth had died naturally whilst in the act of making love. None of them perished until they had changed their wills making him the sole beneficiary: £4.8 million so far he had managed to gain and £4.6 million he had managed to spend.

Rufus and June spent the final eight days of the cruise together, some nights in his cabin, more nights in hers, which was the better appointed. Most nights they danced: those lessons had come in useful after all. Days were spent sightseeing, or relaxing. June felt comfortable with Rufus and flattered by his attentiveness, but Rufus was beginning to panic: they only had one more day and two nights aboard before returning home. He was going to have to make the move which he always liked the woman to make. Still they were on board a ship and the captain was allowed to perform certain ceremonies. He would do it tonight.

He arranged for a table for just the two of them, and after a meal that surpassed even the ship's high standards (it was amazing what a five hundred dollar tip could do) he produced a box from his pocket. He had gone ashore ahead of her two days ago; June was supposed to think that that had been for this purchase, but he had actually brought the ring from home; it had been used more than once. He had stolen one of her rings and sold it to pay for the alterations.

June's face lit up as he opened the box, got down on one knee and uttered the four words, "will you marry me?" The room had gone quiet, all the other diners holding their collective breath waiting for the answer. With a flush to her face and a flutter to her heart that made her feel sixteen again June quietly answered "Yes." Rufus leapt up in excitement; he kissed her and whispered in her ear "I need a quick word with the captain."

He wasn't gone for long, but whilst he was gone many of the other cruisers came over to June to say how pleased they were and how exciting it was. When he came back he pulled June to her feet and led her over to the where the captain was standing. "I understand that this young man has asked you to marry him and that you'd like me to carry out the ceremony tonight. I can do that if you are both sure."

"We are," Rufus answered for both of them.

June was too stunned to speak; she had agreed to marry him, but she didn't think he meant right now. After a brief pause to think about it whilst the captain watched her, she nodded her approval: after all she'd never lived dangerously and if it turned out to be a disaster she could always divorce him.

For the remainder of that night and the following day on board they were treated like royalty. They were given one of the best cabins for their last two nights on board and June found Rufus to be a vigorous and attentive lover.

Once back on shore June found that things weren't quite as she imagined. After Rufus had moved his belongings into her house he insisted that she change her will leaving everything to him and demanded to be present whilst it was done. He assured her that he would do the same with his. As well as spending her money Rufus stayed out many nights claiming, "it's just business darling." The nights he was in he drank to excess and was boorish and ignorant. He'd make demands in the bedroom that left her feeling dirty and unfulfilled; he was a completely different person to the one she'd met on the ship. She decided to do some investigating of her own into this person.

It proved remarkably easy once she had got the thread. She found out what an amazing tool the Internet is. After a few weeks she discovered that Rufus was his real name and that he had been married and widowed five times. She discovered that he owned a harbour-side penthouse apartment and had no active employment. She also found out to her horror that they were not legally married. It was this last fact that annoyed her the most and helped her decide her course of action.

The next time he was with her June quietly mentioned that she had her will with her, "and you remember darling how you said that I would become your sole beneficiary? Well I thought that perhaps tomorrow we could go to my solicitor and do that; then we could lodge both our wills with the probate office." It was her turn to fail to mention something: that she had left an envelope with her solicitor to be opened on her 'sudden or unexpected death'. It contained written evidence of all she had discovered, knowing that the police would find it interesting. After much cajoling and the threat that her handbag would remain shut if it didn't happen, Rufus reluctantly agreed. Then it was just a case of waiting.

Her chance came when he was snoring drunkenly one night and she took his keys from his jacket. She left early the next morning to have them all copied. They were back in his pocket before he had even woken up.

She hired a car and sat outside his apartment block waiting until she knew he was out, then she let herself in. It was tidier than she thought it would be, he must have a cleaner. She was slightly dismayed but not overly surprised to see feminine toiletries in the bathroom. The kitchen had more appliances than hers; she doubted he knew how many of them worked. She let herself out onto the terrace and stared open mouthed at the hot tub that sat there. She decided that as she didn't know how long she'd have to wait she might as well enjoy it. In the fridge she found a bottle of Cristal Champagne and there were two glasses in the dishwasher - no surprise there then; taking them out to the terrace she stripped down to her underwear and climbed into the tub.

She was not sure how long she waited, she could only guess at about half an hour, when the sound of the front door shook her from her reverie. She waited a little longer, counting slowly to thirty, then called "out here darling". After a few moments Rufus's head appeared around the edge of the terrace door.

"Oh hi," he replied somewhat cautiously, "what are you doing here?"

"It's not nice to keep secrets Rufus, especially from your wife. Why don't you come and have a drink with me then we can really have a chat."

"I don't think that's a good idea," he replied. "Look why don't you get dressed and go home, I'll talk to you later." Rufus appeared calm but underneath he was panicking.

June now got angry. She pulled herself from the tub and advanced on Rufus. "You are nothing but a cheap con-man, how I ever got taken in by you I'll never know."

"Oh darling you're so wrong, I maybe a con-man, but I am most definitely not cheap. Why do you think I latched on to you? Because you've got something I want, plenty of cash and property to sell. Oh yes something I forgot to mention, our marriage was only legal whilst we were on that ship, funny that isn't it?"

Rufus grabbed hold of June and began to push her away from him towards the edge of the terrace. "I think now would be the right time for your accident."

There was a brief struggle at the edge of the terrace followed by a scream and a dull thud as a body landed in the communal area eight floors below.

June peered over the edge and smiled to herself, "it's amazing how slippery water is. I think I'll keep this place, I like it. Thank you Rufus and goodbye."

Birthday

Isn't anticipation always more exciting than the reality at the end? That is why I am extremely particular about the wrapping of presents. The crisp, virgin paper that I insist is rolled - no folding - is placed in the middle of the table. I lay my palms in the middle of the cool surface and run them outwards and back to the centre three times. Only then do I begin to wrap the present. I cannot abide irregular presents - they completely ruin the effect.

Now, after years of struggling, I make sure that if it is not easy to wrap it is put in a box. It has taken me a few years but I can now wrap as efficiently as a Bond Street shop girl, but with more precision. The effort is worth it. You can see that from the present on the table. Its hospital corners are encased in a wide blue taffeta ribbon, gathered in an elegant bow on the top. No swirls and definitely no Sellotape visible. I've signed the card "Love from Mum".

I wonder though, son, will you remember this? The effort and care taken even in the wrapping. It amuses me to try and guess what you will remember of your birthdays. Such a myriad of expected festivities: a protocol set down by the Mums of your friends from an early age. Bouncy castles and ice creams for toddlers, which would soon give way to Quasar and football parties. Each mother expected to come up with something bigger, better or different. When those days pass in a whirl of gangly legs, dirty rugby gear and spotty chins you will arrange your own celebrations.

Those teenage nights wandering town centres after the pubs shut with your bottle of Stella, chips and curry sauce in hand, disappearing into elegant dinner parties. The milestones of your years celebrated with the unexpected appearance of friends long gone from your daily life.

Would you feel the excitement when another bright June day dawns? What will I get? Will there be any surprises? I know life's pressures may bear on you - your responsibilities as a father and husband, perhaps, of running a life surrounded by those dependant on you for all their needs. Yet I hope deep inside is a tousled haired six year-old, impatiently jumping on the bed eager to have his breakfast in bed – a special birthday treat to get excited about, though never really liked.

I hope you would not be disappointed when my instinct let me down and I had not bought that one special item you so wanted. Would that bike never ridden, or football kit never worn, remain with you as you grew into a man? A childhood disappointment never fulfilled – regret lasting a lifetime. I pray not.

There would be times you would resent our interference. What sixteen year old wants Mum checking the cocktail sausages and pizzas? A man of twenty-two embarking on, what he hopes, is a really 'hot date' wants to be in the pub boasting about the intended conquest not having high tea with old parents. I'm sure you'll forgive me, though, once your sons come along. You may, too, experience the joy. The innocent elation as the square box, once devoid of it's wrapping, becomes a tank or a CD player or a gun. When you were very small the box itself was the whole world to your young eyes.

It is the celebration of your birth; it should be expected every year on the 6 June. To some it is "just another day", yet how do the sum of all these special days remain with us?

I remember clearly my fourth birthday because I had a Donny Osmond cake and your Auntie burst into tears because I would not let her blow out the candles. Is there a special recollection of one birthday that you could hold up and scrutinise? Are memories only the best of the rest - the best present you ever got as a boy; the best magician; the best trip out; the best rave you ever went to; the best guest to a party?

As I again check the present on the table before me I ponder – you would never know the care and love put into this perfect gift before me. I pray that you will know how my every fibre filled this box with all the love I would never express. Every kiss in the soft place on the side of your neck, every soft stroke of a velvet cheek, every cuddle with small arms grasping tightly round

Birthday

my neck — all are encased in this taffeta bow. I hope that you will remember only this birthday present, this first one, for this birthday you never saw.

Is Earth Ready?

"**O**uch!" moaned FRAM. "You could've made a better landing than that. The whole craft shook, and look at the angle we are standing at. One of our pads must be off any sort of firm surface."

"Oh come on FRAM, that didn't hurt. You don't have any touch sensation sensors so you won't have any bruises," I teased.

FRAM is my Friendly Robotic Atmosphere Module and she adjusts my gas levels between carbon dioxide, nitrogen and oxygen to make sure I am breathing the correct balance to survive on planets alien to Ennorian. We Ennorians are nitrous oxygen absorbers, which makes our outer skin compatible with carbon dioxide, and therefore FRAM's job is essential for us to investigate space and hyperspace. I am Yuli, a feminine Ennorian with very short arms and legs, a body the same length as my legs, and my outer covering is a pale lilac colour. Our common physical attribute with human beings is a brain and we have hearing holes and seeing holes in our skin; we sense smells and absorb nutrients through our membrane, and communicate by a voice box in our speech hole.

FRAM cranked herself out of the security fixing used for skycraft takeoffs and landings, and she went to the vault exit.

"Put on your inhaler Yuli," she instructed. "I'm going to expose us to the outer atmosphere."

"OK. Ready when you are." I replied. She opened the hatch.

"Pooh!" she exclaimed. "Are you sure we're on Planet Earth? The smell out here is horrendous. There is a very high level of methane gas and the dust is worse than on the Moon. I think you should activate TASSIM to see what sort of indications he gives on the outside landscape."

She trundled back into the craft and closed the vault door.

"Oh, that's better," I sighed. Despite using the apparatus for years, I was relieved to close off my inhaler and breathe normally. When FRAM was in the vault-hole I noticed that there was no light; it was coal black all round. I wondered where we were but did not tell my robot companions about my concern.

TASSIM is my Taste and Sensory Indicator Module, and he tells me if he considers we are in a safe area. His reactor told me he was not too happy about where I had landed. I could not understand why he was not comfortable with our situation because I had taken a guide to land from three straight lines of orange lights which I was sure indicated a runway. I must admit that I had to adjust my co-ordinates a bit because when I neared the planet I spotted small white blobs which seemed to be travelling at speed between the lights; presumably these were the lights of craft used to travel the planet internally.

"I'll wait until we have external light before exploring the outside," I told my chums. "Please can you both get my breathing and sensory reactions sorted out so that I don't make a fool of myself if I meet a Being." I switched on LARF (Language Adjusting Robot Friend) and charged up his battery to ensure no breakdown in external communications. I keyed in English but knew that LARF would automatically adjust if I was not on Earth, and closed my eyes to take a little rest before TASSIM told me the Sun had lit up the planet.

"Ping, ping, ping, ping." TASSIM was having trouble waking me from my sleep. I had been more tired from the journey than I realised.

"I'm ready to go," I said, yawning and stretching.

TASSIM opened the vault exit and FRAM adjusted my gas levels. I clipped FRAM onto my belt and attached the ear piece to its centre near my brain. As I stepped out I could not believe what I saw or smelled. I thought Earth was going to be a beautiful green lush planet with running water: instead I was greeted by dirt, piles of crumpled metal and unmentionable rubbish. I cannot describe the smell other than this must be the odour of putrid flesh described in Earth reading matter I had accessed on the Spacenet; it made me cough it was so awful. As I started to absorb my surroundings I heard screeching overhead and saw things that looked like white tubes with extensions each side that moved up and down keeping them airborne. These creatures were swooping down on me. My information clicked in and told me these were birds called seagulls but I could see no sea or water of any kind. Why were they here?

My feet dragged through the material on the ground and stirred up more dust and I was in the mess right up my legs. The smell of the gas increased as the rubbish was moved.

"I really don't like this," I thought.

"Neither do we," projected FRAM and TASSIM. I forgot my thoughts would be transferred automatically to them and my Director because I was keyed in to LARF.

As I turned to go back to the skycraft I heard noises behind me.

"Oi. Who are you and what're you doin'?" A huge Being was calling. He was blue with a bright yellow top half and a black head with a long trunk. I came up to where his body bent and I was terrified.

"Where am I? Is this Planet Earth?" LARF had kicked in and as I spoke in one of their 'normal' voices the Being looked much less threatening. My circulation mechanism slowed down and I began to gain a bit of confidence. The pressure in my brain also diminished.

"Of course it's Earth. Have you come from Outer Space?" laughed the Being. Then he saw my skycraft parked at its rakish angle behind a pile of trash and he gasped. "You *are* from another Planet! George, Rick, come and see what I've found." And he started to stride towards me.

I tried to scramble quickly back to my craft but my extremities are so short that it was impossible to hurry. He was beginning to look threatening again and was gaining on me. I was frightened of this Being who I assumed must be a human being.

"Don't be afraid," he called. "We won't harm you but you must get out of here. We wear these masks to protect us from the dangerous germs and smells." His voice, though muffled, sounded kinder. "Can you take a short trip in that machine? Our work hut, where it's safe, is over there." He pointed to a shiny silver building with a black top and a tube with mist coming out of it – it looked almost like an Ennorian edifice but was much smaller.

I went back to the craft and climbed in. TASSIM greeted me. He had been testing the sensations of the atmosphere, and FRAM had sent a high level tester up into the higher atmosphere. They both confirmed that where the Being had told me to go appeared to be much safer than where we were standing. I asked them if they thought I should meet the humans or we should escape.

"What are you going to tell the Director when we return if you've not even tried to make contact with the aliens? You won't be allowed out on your own again," advised FRAM. "If we receive a fright reaction from you we'll alert your Ennorian Scanner for help. The rescuers will be here with the speed of light because we have already transmitted our co-ordinates."

I took a deep breath and decided to proceed with my assignment but I would not meet the Beings without taking my zapper to dematerialise them if I felt jeopardised. I hoped this would not be necessary because the reason for my mission was to form the basis for links between Ennoria and Earth.

"Rick, go and make a cuppa," ordered the Being who had spoken to me. "We can look on it as a pipe of peace" he laughed.

"OK Fred," called Rick from the doorway of a green building which resembled a picture of a shed I had seen on the Spacenet. "Does she like sugar d'you think?"

"No idea. Ask her!" was the reply.

"My name is Yuli," I called. "And yes, I am the reproductive type of our world — what you call female. Why did you assume I was such?" I questioned.

"Oh on Earth most women take the lead and boss us men about!" answered George.

By now we had reached the green hut and I went inside. On the table there were four of what appeared to me to be large containers; apparently these white things contained the 'cuppa' — whatever that might be. As my thoughts transferred to LARF he translated 'cuppa' as a drink called tea. 'Do I like sugar?' I thought and LARF replied in the negative.

"No sugar thank you," I instructed Rick as he was heating a utensil which had what appeared to be a cloud being forced out of a tube: FRAM told me the cloud was steam, generated by very hot water. I was slowly learning these alien words.

"What is that awful smell outside?" I asked George.

"You've landed on what we call a landfill site," was the answer. "The smell is rotting rubbish and down underneath this are pockets of methane gas which are released through those metal chimneys over there." George pointed through a space filled with clear stuff.

"That's a window and you are looking through glass," supplied LARF.

As George and I talk I can hear Rick and Fred whispering behind us. FRAM turns up the volume on my hearing sensors.

"What a coup!" breathes Rick. "If we can get her in a cage of some kind we'll make a mint at meets like Bridgwater Fair."

"Oh come on man," replies Fred. "She means us no harm and I want no part in doin' som'att like that. 'Sides we dunno wha' we cl'd be messin' with."

"Danger. Danger. Danger," repeats TASSIM. "They're not ready for us yet. Earth is not developed enough to accept different species from other planets. We'll have to come back in about five hundred Earth years."

"Can't I try a bit longer?"

"No. The Director has scanned my readings and wants you to come straight back to the craft," hurries TASSIM.

As I clasp my zapper and swing round to cover the room Rick and Fred are moving towards me; too late they try to grab me. The ethereal rays pour out of the gun and the three men drop to the floor. They are not dead but they will wake with terrible headaches in two days time — the 6th June according to FRAM. We shall be home by then breathing and talking normally. I waddle back to the craft and enter my clean silver capsule with relief. As we rise into the atmosphere we are followed by a black mushroom shaped cloud: presumably we disturbed the methane gas.

Demelza

It was the summer of 1913 and the country was basking in warmth and ignorance; warmth from the perfect unbroken sunshine, ignorance of the horror that would be unleashed the following year. But my life was to change before that, before the war that they said would end all wars. The change came about with just two words, two words spoken by a stranger that would make me question not only who I was, but what I was. It was July and I had just turned thirteen in the June; an only child, I craved company of my own age. I was to have it, but at a price.

We managed the farm, my mother and I, with the help of Jacob, a simpleton with a good heart and a strong back. My mother always seemed careworn, her shoulders stooped, lines of suffering etched into her walnut skin. During my childhood years I recall many times seeing her heavy and swollen, her coarse shift stretched tight across her belly. The midwife would come and I would be sent to the scullery, aware that something was wrong but never told what horror was making my mother keen and wail, like the cows in the field when their calves were taken from them. There were no babies, no playmates to ease the tedium of my life. Sometimes I would go to the dump where the stillborn calves were left and look for those lost babies, but I only ever saw pathetic half-formed animals, discarded and left to rot whilst their mothers bellowed.

My father was a dour man who toiled from sunrise to sundown, seldom acknowledging me. At suppertime we would sit in silence eating bread and cheese, or sometimes a slice of home-cured ham with fat the colour of butter. I loved his farmer's hands, tanned and strong, fingernails caked red from the good earth. I longed to take these hands and press them to my face, feel the hard, calloused skin and smell the rich soil and tell him that I loved him. I never did and then it was too late. He died without warning in the winter of my tenth year. Jacob found him in the barn and I watched him carry the lifeless body to the house. He looked more contented in death than he had in life.

My mother mourned his passing and wore black until the day she died. There were no more visits from the mid-wife, and for that she must have been grateful. On the death of my father, what little schooling I received stopped and my life followed a pattern of monotonous toil which was strangely comforting.

And then came the summer of 1913.

It was an afternoon in July and I was lying on my back in the bottom meadow, counting the clouds that hung in the sky like a flock of heavenly sheep, when I heard shouts coming from the lane. It was Jacob's voice, it held an urgency that caused me to jump to my feet and run towards him.

"Strangers Miss, in top meadow," he panted and we ran quickly to the farmhouse. Mother was churning butter, her face red with effort, her knuckles white on the rough handle.

I shouted, "Mother, Jacob says there are strangers camped in the top field..." A shadow moved across her face as she stopped what she was doing, "Gypsies," she shivered. "It'll be gypsies."

She reached for me and held me close to her. I could feel her heart thudding against her ribs.

"Keep away child, they are thieves, liars and cheats, every one of them. Promise me!" She was shaking me and I began to cry. Relaxing her grip she passed a hand across her forehead. "Finish the churning Liza," and she walked slowly out of the scullery.

The repetitive motion of the churning calmed me. I wondered why my mother hated gypsies so. I had seen villagers cross themselves when they spoke of gypsies, some even spat on the ground, grinding their spittle into the earth as if to add weight to the curse.

That night I dreamed that the gypsies came, their eyes glowing red as blood. They set fire to our farm with flaming torches.

The next day I had finished my chores by noon and I wandered down to the bottom meadow, to lie in my favourite spot in the sweet smelling grass, the buzzing bees for company, the sky a blue canopy over my head. I was dozing and awoke to the sound of laughter. Dazzled by the sunlight, I could see a dark shape above me, and shading my eyes I saw that it was a girl. She looked to be slightly younger than me but with the same dark curls, except that hers had been oiled and they shone like burnished snakes. I sat upright, embarrassed that a stranger had crept up on me. I could see her more clearly now and she seemed to me as beautiful as a Bird of Paradise. Her clothes were the colours of the rainbow and she had hoops of gold threaded through her lobes. She sat beside me and asked my name. When I told her she cocked her head to one side and smiled, her teeth gleaming like pearls in her honey-skinned face.

"I am Demelza," she said, as if this exotic name was as ordinary as Sarah or Jane, or Liza.

Lying down she signalled for me to do the same. In her sweet, lilting voice she held me mesmerized with tales of her life as a gypsy. She enthralled me with tales of the strange and exotic, and she laughed at my ignorance and disbelief.

When the heat of the afternoon sun began to cool she ran away from me, the bare soles of her feet flashing white. I watched her until she was a speck in the distance and I wished that I were running with her.

I dared not tell my mother about Demelza, instead I went out of my way to be helpful. That night as I climbed up to my cot, she caught hold of my hand, "You're a good girl Liza," she said.

I wept in the darkness at my wickedness.

I didn't see Demelza for many days, and I began to believe that she had been an apparition of my own conjuring. When she did appear she came skipping through the grass, curls shimmering in the sunlight, her apron filled with freshly picked daisies. We sat together in companionable silence, splitting each frail stem until our fingers were stained green with the juice. We threaded the delicate stems through the slits, and when they were done, we wound the garlands around our heads and paraded like fairy princesses. As Jacob passed by us in the lane, we curtsied and blew him kisses, laughing at his blushes. He went home and told my mother.

She was waiting for me, her face full of rage, eyes bright with unshed tears. "I warned you child," and I felt the sting of her hand.

I wept and pleaded, but her red rage cooled to steely resolve.

"They are thieves, liars and cheats, you will never see her again."

But Demelza would not give me up. She came for me and together we slipped away. Skirting the barn we ran through the woods and up to the top field.

The kaleidoscope of colours and the cacophony of sounds that greeted me took my breath away. Brightly painted caravans formed a circle inside which a multitude of people were laughing and shouting; children were crying; dogs barking; sounds of music and clapping filled the air. It was all so wild and wonderful. Demelza took my hand and led me to a caravan set apart from the rest. "You must see Grandmother," and she pushed me up the wooden steps and through a curtain of glass beads that sparkled like water falling down a sunlit waterfall. The old woman before me was dressed in black velvet, a scarf knotted around her head, a string of coins upon her forehead.

"Come child, sit," and she motioned to a stool at her feet.

She looked into my eyes and something stirred within me. She touched my curls and smiled, "They should be oiled," her voice was rich with an accent unknown to me. "Your mother is well child?" I nodded, not knowing why she would ask. "Your father will want to know." I found my voice, "He's dead, my father is dead." She took my hand and looked again into my eyes, "Your father is alive my child, he is here, he is my son." The only sound I heard was the beating of my heart as I stared at this stranger. What could she mean, this old crone with her ridiculous clothes and foolish drivel? I stood, knocking over the stool in anger. I was desperate to get out, away from this gaudy caravan and these people with their ragamuffin children, mangy dogs and suffocating campfires. I needed to go home to my mother and tell her that she was right and that I would never, ever disobey her again. Just as I parted the bead curtain, just as I was about to escape, I heard the old woman whisper. I turned back, a clawed hand gripping my heart, "What did you say?" my voice thin and strangled, not like my own. With a look half pitying, half triumphal, she stretched out her hands to me, "The 6th June; you were born on the 6th June, thirteen years ago." And in that moment I knew she spoke the truth.

The Harvest Hymn

The Reverend Lucifer Humble moved closer to the lectern and nodded in the direction of frail, partially deaf, one-legged church organist Dr Peregrine Lovejoy.

"Let us unite," said the Reverend, smiling and clasping his hands together as he addressed the congregation, "and sing together the traditional harvest hymn 'We Plough the Fields and Scatter the Good Seed on the Land'. And as we sing this joyous anthem of thanksgiving for the bounteous offerings here before us, we should remember those less fortunate."

The Reverend paused, seeking maximum effect. Peregrine Lovejoy anticipated this to be the cue he had been awaiting. He turned to face the organ, fiddled with his ear-piece and, with commendable enthusiasm, pounded out the opening chords, taking the Reverend completely by surprise.

The choir and congregation rose as one and set off in pursuit of Peregrine's opening salvo. The startled Reverend looked anxiously towards the choir, in particular the balding, portly, figure of Arthur Cockle, who for some weeks had been experiencing great difficulty achieving the higher notes. The choir, resplendent in white smocks, appeared unperturbed as their lead tenor, his eyes bulging from their sockets, cheeks flushed with effort, fought to attain the upper reaches, whilst simultaneously attempting to maintain pace with his fellow choristers.

Lucifer transferred his gaze from the struggling tenor; his eyes eventually settling upon the radiantly blooming figure of Fiona Promiss, who, obligingly, looked up and smiled sweetly as Lucifer, arms flailing wildly, sought to unite choir and congregation in their endeavour to draw abreast of Peregrine's racing organ.

"All good things around us are sent from Heaven above."

The vociferous gathering sailed through this section almost in unison, allowing Lucifer to relax a little and fantasise over his dear sweet Fiona. He vividly recalled their first meeting on a wet Wednesday evening – June 6th 2002 – was it really that long ago? Lucifer had been preaching to the 'Young People's Fellowship', joyfully extolling the virtues of a happy marriage and the unique pleasure of 'coming together in the name of the Lord.' It was at this point that Fiona had giggled, the first time he'd really noticed her. It was all so clear, seeming like only yesterday, yet here they were, a little over a year on and Fiona heavy with child – his child. What would the austere blue-rinsed Winifred, his wife of twenty-seven years, make of it all if she were ever to stumble across the pottering mild-mannered vicar she so dominated at home, rattling the long grass in the neglected 'Garden of Tranquillity', with a girl barely a third of his fifty-three years. Lucifer preferred instead to think of the many picnics he'd enjoyed with Fiona. How they laughed long into the evenings, the carefree Lucifer sitting on a tin of golden syrup, his legs kicking out uncontrollably as he watched in awe the delicate Fiona dance the 'Sugar Plum Fairy' on top of the picnic hamper (teasing him with her blueberry muffins), allowing him just an occasional nibble.

Lucifer also shared with Fiona a love of the garden and he recalled the unbridled ecstasy he experienced as they feverishly worked off the stresses of the day, safe in the secluded sanctity of the herbaceous borders. He reflected upon the occasion she had mockingly admonished him for startling her by slipping in through her back entrance when it would have been easier to enter at the front.

Lucifer gave a wry smile.

"Dear God forgive me, for I know I have sinned," he muttered quietly to himself. "The lure of Fiona's muffins will remain with me for ever and ever – Amen. Just once more, O Lord, and I vow never again shall I trespass along the path of unrighteousness."

Police Sergeant Norman Duff's booming baritone suddenly thundered from the rear of the church: a clear indication that he had finally arrived at the correct page in his 'Songs of Praise' hymn book. Lucifer was shaken from his day dreams and the choir, floating serenely in the upper echelons of the harvest hymn, was throw completely off course. The baffled choristers looked in vain to their leader for guidance, but Arthur Cockle was entrapped in his own tenorial world, two notes behind Sergeant Duff and losing ground fast. The exuberant sergeant quickly established a sizeable lead over the congregation until, much to their great relief, his spirited contribution began to wane, his thoughts drifting back to the station, where he had left constables Pillfering and Tamper checking out their new bicycles, the complexity of the Sturmy-Archer gear system a problem that was already proving to be a bridge too far for the hapless duo.

A strange, ethereal, sound began to emanate from Peregrine's old organ and he frantically pushed, pulled, twiddled and twirled the ancient stops in an attempt to rejoin the fray. Just when all seemed lost, the old organ burst back into life with a bizarre version of what appeared to the Christian gathering to be a combination of the harvest hymn interposed with short passages from 'Abide With Me', bringing much joy and thanksgiving to a bewildered congregation.

Sergeant Duff, having dropped well off the pace - his thoughts elsewhere - had been replaced at the forefront of the vocal assault by the battling choir, closely followed by the congregation, who, in turn, were trailed by Arthur Cockle. The congregation shifted and shuffled uneasily, unsure which path to follow. Should they reduce pace and stay with Arthur or forge ahead with the rest of the choir? A fifty-fifty split appeared to be the agreed compromise as the divided gathering set off along their chosen paths.

Meanwhile, the old organ, despite frantic pumping from Peregrine's good leg, had lost considerable ground and was now chasing the pack with little hope of catching them as the 'Amen' drew ever closer. The choir, together with one half of the congregation, were first to register the 'Amen'.

Arthur Cockle, though temporarily rejuvenated, had since faded and lost his way, taking the remnants of the gathering with him, finishing in disarray as he and his followers began to realise the opposition had already reached their destination.

United at last, the whole church awaited the arrival of Peregrine Lovejoy's troublesome organ. The old master eventually struck the final chord and turned to face the gathering, a broad, contented, smile creasing his craggy face. He bowed his head slightly and brushed a few wisps of thin grey hair from his perspiring forehead. There was a spluttering of applause from a few of the older members of the congregation, some of whom could remember far back in time to the halcyon days when Peregrine was invariably first to close in on the 'Amen'. He milked the sparse applause for a while before turning to face his beloved instrument, ready, willing and questionably able to tackle the next assignment. He flicked through the well-worn pages of his sheet music, arriving eventually at 'Nearer My God To Thee', slower and much more to his liking. He glanced up at the beleaguered Lucifer in anticipation and awaited his cue. Lucifer nodded and smiled fondly at his old friend. Peregrine fiddled with his ear-piece once more and placed his gnarled, shaky old hands on the keyboard in readiness for the task ahead.

The Reverend Lucifer Humble moved closer to the lectern...

Arab Image

"I'm telling you, he did! Please sir, can I have my money?"
Russell looked at the boy uncertainly. "How, exactly, did he
disappear?"

The small child rattled Arabic off at too great a speed and full of too
many colloquialisms for Russell to fully comprehend.

"What do you mean he just appeared and then disappeared? Talk slower!
How did he appear?"

For once in his young life, Tariq was being almost completely truthful.

"He...he just was there. And he spoke to the men. And then he wasn't
there."

He merely neglected to mention that he had been too afraid of discovery
to edge that extra metre closer to quite see around the corner. That small
couple of steps that would have magnified all understanding to form actual
enlightenment in the mind of his temporary master. Those extra steps that
would have lead to wonder rather than the mundane, curiosity as well as
simple fear.

Russell sighed. "Look, here's three."

"You said five!" The child practically screamed at the injustice of the
Westerner. "You said five!"

Russell looked about him in alarm lest an adult spotted his furtive
bargaining and jumped to murderous conclusion. The Arabs within the
Jerusalem province of the newly instituted Republic of Palestine weren't
noted for their tolerance of Americans.

"Look. Just be quiet. I didn't say I wouldn't pay you, I want you to do
some more work for me, that's all." Russell was tight-lipped. "Here's an
imager. Keep it beneath your caftan until you see the man come back and
then just point it in the rough direction of the man and press the button."

"Yes, yes I've used one before – in a shop!" The boy's eyes were aglow.
He seemed a little too enthused by his new present for Russell's liking. He

half expected to see it on sale in the souk before the boy had added too many minutes to his tender years.

"Follow the men when they leave again. Only use the imager when the man's with them. Got it? It's only got a small memory: it can't take more than about ten minutes OK?" He was deliberately kinder. "I'll pay you the other two when you come back and another ten if the pictures have got the man on." Russell gambled that he'd provided sufficient incentive, together with the prospect of further earnings, to ensure the return of the imager.

"Do you understand?"

"Yes, yes. Take pictures of the man." The boy examined the image display minutely; marvelling at the brief holovid he'd captured of himself, wide grin and smiling eyes included. The hologram was perfectly centred, even though he'd thrown the instrument extensively to either side. He laughed a child's laugh and, for a brief second, Russell saw the cynical adult dissolve from the boy's eyes to reveal uncaring innocence. Russell, however, had no time for such indulgence. He was still unconvinced that the boy genuinely comprehended his instructions, distracted as Tariq was by the technological treasure that he grasped. Russell made Tariq repeat the instructions to his latest mission in true military fashion.

Tariq peeped around the corner of the house down the narrow alley, through the curtain of dust woven by the sunlight. A whiff of petrol from a primus stove tugged at his nostrils. This, and the crazy twisting of the walls and their attendant shadows, meant a move closer than he would have wished towards the small group of men.

Bleached robes swept the pentagonal paving. Impressive jewellery dripped from fingers that held thin, dirty, cigarettes. Tariq knew that if he was caught he risked at least a thorough beating and his quick, shallow breathing reflected his caution. Tariq decided on an experiment. He fiddled with the holovid beneath his clothes until it was held against the outermost linen of his voluminous garments. He nonchalantly slipped from concealment and walked right up to one of the group.

"Please sir, have you seen my brother?"

"No, no. Go away," said the man with obvious irritation. "I'm busy. I haven't seen anyone. Be off!" He gesticulated, but was too slow for Tariq, who just managed to duck the man's flailing hand and leave it to meet only with the thick, oppressive, air. He feigned fright and retreated to his vantage point.

He quickly pulled the technological marvel from amongst his garb and flipped out the view screen. To his delight he found that the taught linen just above his belt had reduced the image quality only marginally, merely introducing a slight fogging, although the bright sun eradicated the scene towards the top of the hologram.

Tariq kept behind his "hard cover", as he'd heard some of the older boys call it, periodically risking a swift glance towards the group but ultimately deciding that it was better to brave the danger of discovery than to miss the coming of the stranger that his employer was so keen to witness.

He turned towards the group once more, regarding them with one eye, in the manner familiar to so many of his generation and their fathers.

A ball of the purest white light began to glow above the group. Tariq's mouth visibly dropped, his brow knitting. He momentarily forgot how precarious was his position and stepped forward, away from the wall, his gaze held as if he were lead by a ring through his nose. The ball elongated and slowly descended perpendicular to the ground. The group became aware of the presence of the phenomenon but simply fell silent and moved respectfully away, extinguishing tobacco and straightening clothing. The pearlescent glow slowly brightened from within, with a pure jet slither of nothing piercing perfection. And then he came. He simply stepped through this radiant cat's eye from a still hazardous height and was immediately among the group, greeting down-turned eyes with smiles and laughter and offering his hands to eager kisses.

Tariq had momentarily lost all sense of who, or where, he was. He managed to remember the holovid concealed beneath his gown and, realising that he might easily be seen, withdrew it once again after he had hurriedly scuttled back to his burrow. He continued to image the scene as the man chatted and nodded with the others. A hand was lain on the shoulder of a burly and distinct individual who nodded and then left the group by way of another of the myriad of streets that formed the capillaries of the city. Arms were gripped by hands as the group split, cheeks were kissed and then the man turned and walked back into the darkness within the light. The elongated light, still buoyant, having never made contact with the ground, retracted into a ball once more and then rapidly span, disappearing into it's own centre.

Tariq shuffled further into the dimness as two of the group walked past, obviously enjoying one another's company. Once he was sure that there was no one in the vicinity, Tariq flipped open the view screen and checked his recent handiwork. Pleased with the results, the young cameraman secreted the imager into his belt once more and prepared to leave the relative safety of the shadows.

"What were you doing? Why are you still here? Did you find your brother?"

Tariq looked up into narrowed eyes that pierced the dinginess around him.

"Well? Come here!"

Tariq had no option, cornered as he was. There would be no clever ducking the back of the man's hand this time.

Drawn face. Hollowed cheeks. An impressively full beard that was strangely cut off square at the bottom. Two small plaits behind the man's ears that Tariq hadn't noticed before. In one horrified moment Tariq realised that the man must be a Jew.

"I . . . I came back. I couldn't find him. I thought I must have missed him. He was playing around here. You haven't seen him have you?" Tariq's calm surprised even himself.

"What did you see here?"

The man's jaw firmed, his mirthless grin revealed gritted, tar-stained, teeth.

"Nothing! Nothing! Honest, I never saw anything. I just came back here! I don't know anything about any bargains! I didn't even see who you were with."

The man's hand tightened on Tariq's arm as he drew him towards him. Tariq smelled stale tobacco as the man whispered directly into his face.

"You saw nothing! There was nobody here and nothing happened! Got it?" Tariq nodded extravagantly. The man's eyes continued to dart over the boy's face and Tariq was compelled to look away.

"Go!"

Tariq required no second bidding and slipped from the man's presence as if he were a pigeon escaping the shadow of a hawk.

Tariq ran and ran hard. Russell was almost rapturous in his praise, but even he failed to grasp what had truly occurred.

A small boy of no importance: the only independent witness to the coming of the Messiah on this day of 14 SHawwal 1441 A.H.

The Messiah of the Jews.

The Messiah of Islam.

The Second Coming.

The Escape

"**S**he's lost the plot completely today."

"Who?"

Shirley jerked her head towards the room she'd just left.

"Edith. Can't get her to do anything. She just keeps saying, 'it's the day, it's the day' over and over again. I don't know what she's on about."

Tina shrugged. "Best to leave them when they're like that. You can't do nothing with them. Come and help me get Irene out of bed."

They moved off, down the shabby corridor with its scuffed skirting boards and cheap, faded prints of sunflowers and poppy fields.

Inside the room Edith stayed in bed until she heard the voices fade away. Then she pushed back the thin duvet and swung her legs round. Now, she said to herself, now, and yanked herself painfully out of bed, pulling on the handrail fixed to the wall.

The room was hot; far too hot. She kept opening the window, which always provoked them, for some reason. "You'll catch a cold Edith, sitting in a draught." What nonsense. Everyone knew colds were a virus, or if they didn't, they ought to.

She drew back the flowery curtains and tried to ease up the sash window, but for some reason it wouldn't budge. Edith examined it more closely. Damn! It was bolted down. They'd locked her window. What on earth was she going to do? Well, she'd outwit them somehow; nothing would stop her today.

Leaning heavily on her wheeled frame, she propelled herself to the white melamine chest of drawers, and pulled open her underwear drawer. Slipping her hand under the scented paper drawer-lining, she felt her fingers close on a small, folded piece of paper. Still there, thank goodness; they hadn't discovered it.

71

Edith rummaged until she found her best stockings and her silk underwear edged with ivory-coloured lace. Important to look her best today. She pulled the fine stockings up and clipped them into place. Her legs had always been slim and shapely. Even mother had admitted she had a well-turned ankle.

As she tucked the note neatly into her brassiere, she could hear her mother's voice.

"Well, that's not very ladylike, Edith."

Nothing was very ladylike in her mother's opinion: running, cycling, wearing bright colours, singing to herself, laughing out loud; all were 'vulgar' and to be frowned on. "Don't draw attention to yourself Edith," was the chief commandment. The aim of a properly-brought-up young lady was to slip through life unnoticed, quietly, escaping society's disapprobation.

Well, she had been noticed. Plain little Edith, as Father called her. Well, not everyone thought she was plain.

Even the horrible net curtains couldn't hide the fact it was a glorious summer's day. A thin petticoat would do beneath her cotton frock. Pale pink rosebuds and a sweetheart neckline. Her favourite, matched with a white belt and cardigan. Eddie like it. Called her his English rose.

Thinking of Eddie made her stomach turn over in a sick, excited sort of way. She'd been too nervous to eat anything last night, or even to have a cup of tea this morning. It didn't matter, they could eat later, at a restaurant.

Her father didn't approve of restaurants.

"No point in spending good money on fancy food when your mother makes a perfectly acceptable dinner. It's indulging in that kind of extravagance that leads to discontent."

Discontent was the second deadly sin. Discontent led one on a headlong descent through evils such as envy and not knowing one's station, right through to truly unforgivable sins such as foreign travel and falling in love.

Edith knew herself to be a hothouse rampant with sins. She'd tried very hard at first to weed out sinful thoughts, praying and fasting and going to both communion and evensong, but they kept springing up. She'd see a pretty girl at church, and feel envy, however hard she pinched herself, and on the way home would run across the road to smell a climbing rose, thus drawing attention to herself. She had to be constantly alert, fighting her wayward impulses. Then, when she met Eddie, she knew it was hopeless. For the first time in her life, she threw her head back and laughed helplessly, until her stomach hurt, and it felt so good that she wanted to go on doing it forever. She abandoned herself to sin.

Just meeting Eddie had been a miracle of good luck. On leave from the R.A.F., he'd been visiting his aunt in the village, and they'd met by chance in the lane leading from her house to the baker's. 'Love at first sight', as the saying went. Edith smiled to herself. She knew it was true.

She applied a little touch of lipstick carefully. A rosebud mouth. What sweet things he always said. On second thoughts, she rubbed it off again. It might draw attention to herself, and it wasn't worth it, not when everything depended on her getting out of the house without arousing any suspicion.

She opened her bedroom door gently. All was quiet apart from some clattering from the kitchen. Hopefully mother was absorbed in her chores.

Edith moved quietly down the corridor towards the front door. How worn the carpet was looking. Gently, gently, don't rush. She could see fresh green leaves in the garden through the mottled glass of the front door now. Her stomach was turning over and over with nerves. Only a few steps now and she would be outside.

Her shaking hand was on the latch. Oh quickly, quickly, she told herself, and pulled gently at the handle, then harder.

Oh, no….no! The door was locked. Oh why, why was it locked? It was never locked except at night. Had they found her out? She looked nervously over her shoulder.

"Edith!"

Oh no.

"Edith, whatever are you doing?"

"Just going for a little walk." Edith tried to keep her voice normal. "But the door's locked."

Matron laughed. "Of course it's locked. We can't have you wandering up the street, can we?"

"I only want to go for a walk." Edith looked through the door at the leaves, yearningly.

"You know that's not possible. Why don't you sit in the lounge with the others? There's a sing-song at eleven -you'd like that. Or would you rather be in your room?"

"I want to go out."

"Now Edith, be a good girl." Matron put a hand on Edith's arm to steer her round. Edith felt desperation gripping at her heart.

"No, no." She began to wail loudly.

Matron tried not to get impatient, but Edith's timing was maddening. Only the Department of Health inspection in an hour's time, and everyone behind schedule already! She exerted a slight pressure on Edith's arm, trying to get her to turn round. Edith began to scream.

Two of the staff appeared.

"Mike, Tina, can you get Miss Holden back to her room please, quickly. She's having a bit of a tantrum. Best make sure she stays there until she's calmed down a bit. Then I'd suggest a little more Amitryp, given our visit this morning."

Edith's feet seemed to leave the ground and she was swept away towards her bedroom, then deposited in the big armchair. As the door closed she heard the click of the lock.

Oh, whatever would she do? There was no time to spare. She struggled up from the chair. Oh, the window, they'd locked the window too. They must have guessed. Oh, Eddie, whatever shall I do?

In the station waiting room Eddie looked at his pocket watch anxiously. Where was Edith? The London train was due in an hour. A clammy hand grabbed hold of his heart. Perhaps she had changed her mind. It was so much to ask of a young girl, to leave home and take a chance with him. He'd not much money either. He couldn't blame her if she'd bottled out. Wretched, he lit another cigarette. Please God, let her come, he prayed. I'll never do anything bad ever in my whole life. I'll look after her forever. He checked his watch again. And again, and again.

Edith feels the glass with her hands, pushing against it. She can see the china blue sky, the perfect green and pink of the magnolia tree. A swallow soars past towards the eaves.

The room is so hot and airless. Outside, a breeze dances through the magnolia leaves, causing a cascade of pink petals to spiral dizzily down onto the grass. A bee staggers drunkenly along the bottom of the window-ledge. Edith presses her cheek against the warm glass. Oh Eddie, Eddie, rescue me.

A sudden pang of desperation stabs at her heart and she begins to beat the window with her fists, sobbing. The warm June sun scorches down pitilessly through the impenetrable window. Edith feels sick and faint. She looks fearfully at the marble clock on her bedside table. Half-past eleven. She must do something quickly, she must get out. The clock, the clock! She seizes the clock, once her grandmother's, a hideous, ugly thing. It feels so cold in her hands, so heavy. She raises her arms, wincing with the effort and throws the clock at the glass.

The crack and shrill splintering of glass.

Edith feels a cool rush of air and the sharp bee-stings in her hands. Someone is crushing her heart, she can't breathe. A darkness closes round her. Oh Eddie.

Running feet.

"Oh, God, what's she done?"

"Quick, get the nurse, get Matron."

Edith's body is motionless. Her face is pale, her eyes closed. Her hands are bandaged; the rose-bud frock and white cardigan, spotted with blood, are sealed in a plastic sack, waiting to be incinerated. Her underwear is in the laundry bin. It will come back to her: both items have Edith Holden written in biro on stiff, scratchy labels inside.

Edith herself will come back, though not for a while, for she has been heavily sedated. When she wakes she will see that the window pane has been replaced, and some additional safety features in the form of narrow iron bars have been added to the inside of the window frame.

The Sixth of June

Shirley, who put Edith to bed, is putting her things in order when she suddenly remembers something. She fishes in her pocket for the piece of paper she'd found tucked, oddly, into Edith's bra when she undressed her.

She's never seen a thinner, more fragile piece of notepaper, grubby and creased, as if it's been folded and unfolded a thousand times. The ink is faint and spidery, but still legible.

Her lips move silently as she reads the note.

"Darling Edith, only a moment to scribble this. I have fixed to come for you on the 6th of June. I will be at the Railway Station at Bigginswade at 11 o'clock, & have booked seats for the 12.15 to Kings Cross. Don't be late my darling, I know it won't be easy but you must manage it somehow. Don't risk bringing any luggage, you might get rumbled. Just come as you are, I will get you what you need in London. I must go my darling, but soon I will have you forever at last. Don't be late – all my love until then, Eddie xxx.

Remember – 6th June."

Sword Beach: 6th June 1944

Tommy squinted down, his head to one side. It was oddly familiar: he knew this crumpled pile of clothing.

"Thou knows ya know!" a voice laughed beside him.

Tommy started, but smiled slightly, vaguely recognising the voice.

"I know?"

"Aye! Thou knows!"

Tommy gazed at his companion uncertainly.

"What do I know corporal?"

The humour was lost to him.

It was his companion's turn to look down at the mess of damp, mangled, cotton and canvas. He said nothing, simply raising his head once more to return Tommy's gaze.

"Would thou like ma to leave ya 'ere for a bit? Just to calm down after the rush up the beach? Relax a bit like?"

"Sure." replied Tommy quietly. He frowned at his Yorkshire brother, knowing only that what was right was wrong and that what was dream was now.

"I'll leave ya for a bit then. I'll just be over the top of that dune when thou decide to finish ya rest."

"Wait!" Tommy almost screamed. He shocked himself with the vehemence of his call. Looking around beneath the beads of sweat that were beginning to sting his eyes, he observed the oasis of quiet that was this small corner of a foreign beach. Suddenly more alone than any lost child had ever been, Tommy grasped at the only straw that presented itself.

"Are there any officers about?" he shouted.

"Aye. Several, over the dune."

Tommy swallowed.

"Is there still fighting that way?"

"Aye," smiled the corporal, "Aye, they's still fighting over that way."

The wind caught at Tommy's blond curls, bleached by sea and summer sun, and playfully tugged at them. He'd had a mass of them on the farm, another life away: he'd vowed, even as they'd hit the barber's shop floor, to grow them once again. Patricia would pull her fingers through those curls as she pulled him to her mouth. Run her fingers through, to deliberately catch them and toy with them as she toyed with him and he with her.

Tommy flipped his helmet into his lap to mop his brow and fished for some ciggies in his breast pocket. He wondered when he'd feel her next to him again. Feel her breast rise against him as their passion overcame their caution. Would she still be there for him? Even in his certainty he was undermined by a twinge of doubt.

"Is she pretty?"

Tommy's only reply was a quizzical frown.

"Yer lass! Is she pretty?"

"Yes. Yes, very pretty," Tommy finally managed, more quietly than he'd intended. "How did you know that I was thinking about Patty?"

"Yer 'ad tha look. Seen that look a thousand times today I 'ave. Were yer goin' ta be spliced?"

"Married? No! Well; not yet a while anyways," finished Tommy, rather lamely.

" 'Not yet a while?'," parroted the corporal. His face hardened. He was not a harsh, nor an unkind soul but some things had to be done.

"Where's yer rifle son?"

"Lost it running up the beach corporal." Tommy's eyes suddenly widened as he realised the enormity of his statement.

"What's that then lad?"

The corporal nodded towards a Lee-Enfield, clip still in place and with bayonet a-fixed, resting on the solid, glistening sand. Tommy regarded the 303 curiously, aware that it really shouldn't be there, but not quite sure where it should be. Eventually limpid thought condensed and hardened from the fog slowly creeping through.

Now, he is in an outdoor room, the sky the ceiling: in the open, yet confined. Tommy gazes upon a vista of unbounded activity. Activity now foreign. Men. Men everywhere. Men rushing forward. Men lying down. Men probing the ground with sticks. A man crumpling to the sand even as his comrades surge around him.

The odd brilliant fire-flash riveting his gaze: the only colour in a canvas washed into bare monochrome by the sea. Above all, grey machines emerging from grey waters, crystallising: one moment fluid, indistinct, the next substantial, present, threat or friend. Changing the occupancy of his thoughts as they crystallise with them.

He's just managed to free himself of the clinging, cloying, embrace of the waters above the knee. He has succeeded in divesting himself of restraint to run freely; a rite of passage. The atavistic scream of the charge has begun to rise in his throat. The sense of the present is overwhelming: there is no future, no past, just himself and the adversary and the fear.

Row upon row of triangular steel sculptures pierce the sand: starkly aesthetic landing craft obstacles, each topped by a mine. Man's contribution, as ever, a scar on the natural. Tommy hoped that they would be gone soon. And finally, the thought.

He would be going with them.

Before was noise, now was quiet. Before was action, now was repose. Before was the zombie automaton of unthinking immediacy. Now was deep reflection.

The war itself had planted fear in Tommy. It had furtively rooted, gradually tightening its hold on an unwitting host. Now this young shoot had aged to maturity. Now was terror.

"Thou are afraid of it 'cause thou 'ave refused to face up to it until now that it's touched thou on tha shoulder."

"No! No! It's not fair! No!"

"Thou'll die harder son if ya don' accept it now! Your wish is father to no thought: never will be!"

The corporal decided to be even more stark. "All euphemisms are lies lad! Thou are just plain bloody dead! There's no sugaring of tha pill. Thou are dead. Live with it!"

The Other Beach

My daughter has taken to asking me why I sit and look at the fall of sunlight across the wall. She's a good girl, Amy. Of course, I shouldn't call her that, she being sixty-three this year with children and grandchildren of her own. But I still think of her as a girl.

A good girl. Never taken me to task for not re-marrying. Comes to see me every week or so, never under duress, bless her, just to see how her old dad is doing and make sure the other inmates aren't driving me crazy. They're OK, of course, some a bit dotty, but all harmless enough.

So, the wall, the sunlight. Once, thinking to keep her happy, I said "It helps me to remember things." And then, quick as a flash, she came back with "Still, I suppose the memories are all you've got left." How that hurt. All. As if somehow they were cheap and second-hand. As if I'd stopped living.

Most likely you will have almost seen me before, perhaps a hundred times or more.

The fragment of film from D-Day, you know the one, with the door of the landing craft dropping, the French beach ahead, a seaside town, a building in the foreground, a shop or a bar, and the troops moving forward into the sea to commence the invasion. I was there, standing just to the left of the cameraman, trying not to jog his elbow as I pushed past and followed the rest of them into that mad future. If you look carefully, you can just see the edge of my sleeve. He did not capture me; he stopped filming as I drew level with him. So I am almost a part of that timeless image, almost. And you may have almost seen me.

Once I told Benny about it - him from the room at the end of corridor – and he said "So what do you remember?" I shrugged. "You know, being afraid, feeling sick, the usual stuff." We left it at that.

In truth it was nothing like that.

I remember that as I stepped forward I was remembering the last time I had seen Joan on leave. Remembering sitting by the fire with her, my arms around her shoulders, her crying quietly. My sister had taken Amy, and Joan and I had spent the afternoon in bed. But all we had done was cling to each other.

I was remembering then when I met her, in the summer of 1940. Lord, what a looker! She was the prettiest thing I had ever laid eyes on. Moved like a gazelle. Quivered with energy and passion. No question, it was lust at first sight. But with love following hard on its heels. When I asked her to marry me, she was having one of her crazy days and she grabbed hold of me and danced me round the room laughing and yelling "Anything to get in my knickers!". She knew.

I knew about her problems before we got married. I'd seen how some days the gloom settled on her, how she sat in the corner of a darkened room and her voice shrank to a whisper. I knew. But I thought "I'll make it right." Some hope.

Once I worked out how long it must have taken. You know, acceleration due to gravity and all that. I reckoned five seconds. How much can you remember in five seconds? Does it all flash past like they say? Or do you remember just one thing with pristine clarity?

So on that last afternoon, she had lain in my arms, shaking and sobbing. I remember saying to her "What is it, darling?" Same stupid bloody question. As if there's an it to know. As if any of it could ever make any kind of sense at all. As if you could fix it with a hammer and screwdriver or blow it apart with a 25 pounder. As if. But she went quiet for a moment, and then said "I can't bear to remember any more. I don't want any more memories. They're crushing me." And then she began to cry again.

On the landing craft, I was so afraid that I nearly shit myself. Several of the blokes were sick. The boat stank like a carsie. When you're that afraid, everything closes in. You stop being a normal human being and you become this container for fear. It fills you, horizon to horizon and seabed to sky. And you want to run. You so want to run, even if it's forward, into the bullets and shellfire. Anything but sit with it. But you have to wait until they drop the ramp. That's the worst time, just before the ramp goes down. You think you will burst open with the fear. That's when I remembered Joan, just as I was pushing past the cameraman, into this future.

That's the only memory that's really mine any more. The problem with being a bit player on such a stage is that everybody else takes your memories as their own. My son-in-law knows more about those landings than me, knows every detail, all the regiments, where the tanks went ashore, who got killed first. He wasn't even there. He was four years old when it happened. But they've taken my memories and made them theirs, so I hardly recognise them any more, me the shadow man, the almost-there man.

What they won't remember is the other beach. Five seconds. Five seconds down from the cliff-edge. Five seconds-worth of memories and then a broken body and nothing more. As I was trudging ashore into the machine-gun fire, Joan was flying through the bright air. My darling Joan.

And now the wall and the sunlight. Pristine.

Rosemarie Ford

After being forced into early retirement through ill health, a friend cajoled me into enrolling for a Creating Writing class. As a secretary/PA in my working life, I have always been renowned for my letters of complaint! By careful nurturing from by our super Tutor I have a new hobby and made new friends. My dream of being in print is fulfilled!

Patricia Golledge

In spite of having won Highly Commended for stories at the Weston Arts Festival Short Story Competition in 2002, 2003 I find it hard to keep up inspiration with a four year old keeping me on my toes. My twelve years in the Foreign Office has given me plenty of material. All I need now is the time!

Peter Goodsall

What it is to be ... somebody, anything, anywhere, else? I've often wondered but until recently never articulated any thoughts. I underwent a personal "Epiphany" during two years of creative writing tutelage and now, for good or ill, can't stop! Oh yes: married with two children, point seven of a dog...

Deborah Grice

When I was six I told my classmates that I was called Georgina Isabel Winter-Taylor, and that my father was a sea captain. Later I found that lying was more socially acceptable when you wrote it down, and decided to make a career of it. All the same, I hope you find some truth in these stories.

Alyson Heap

When my daughter asked if I would go with her to a Creative Writing class I readily agreed, I was always good at essay writing, even if it was 40 years ago! With three grown up children in various stages of flying the nest I needed something to fill the void. Thanks to an inspiring tutor I discovered a hidden 'voice' and writing is now both a hobby and a passion. I can't yet call myself a 'a writer', but who knows, one day...

Martin Mickleburgh

Martin Mickleburgh was born and brought up in the Black Country in the 1950s. He graduated from Loughborough University with a degree in Sociology and Economics in 1973 (draw your own conclusions...). After a short but fruitless stint as a composer of almost serious music, he discovered the gentle art of systems analysis, the practice of which has detained him ever since. His aspirations as a writer took a while to mature - twenty-five years or so - but, once liberated, have taken wing in the form of one and a half novels, several short stories and numerous poems. He does not like cats, much.

Dave Mills

Born in Bristol 1963 the third of five children. Started writing poetry when in his teens, but did not write seriously until into his thirties. He has had three poems and one short story published. He would like to pursue writing permanently and is about halfway through his first novel.

Pete Owen

I was born sixty years ago in Bristol. Educated at a Secondary Modern School, I excelled at sport but little else. My favourite past times are: eating plums; scratching myself when I'm itchy and wearing a pink hat with a bobble on it. I also like to run on the spot sometimes.